CE

 **Walsall** Council

This item is due for return on or before the last date shown.

- Renew your books 24 hours a day
- Find out when your library is open
- Check your Walsall library details

Library-Line: **01922 709256**

On-line Library Services: Follow the link from
www.walsall.gov.uk/libraries

Harir Khobor

What's Cooking in Bengal

Harir Khobor
What's Cooking in Bengal

Gini Sen

New Age Publishers (P) Ltd

LONDON
HYDERABAD ERNAKULAM BHUBANESWAR
DELHI KOLKATA PUNE

NCBA

REGD OFFICE

8/1 Chintamoni Das Lane, Kolkata 700 009, India
email: ncbapvtltd@eth.net

OVERSEAS

NCBA (UK) Ltd, 149 Park Avenue North, Northampton, NN3 2HY, UK

EXPORT

NCBA Exports Pvt. Ltd, 212 Shahpur Jat, New Delhi 110 049
email: ncbaexp@ncbapvtltd.com

BRANCHES

208B Peacock Lane, Shahpur Jat
New Delhi 110 049
email: ncbadel@ncbapvtltd.com

House No. 3-1-315, 1st Floor
Nimboliadda, Kachiguda, **Hyderabad** 500 027
email: ncbahydb@ncbapvtltd.com

Shop Nos. 3 & 4, Vinayak Towers
681/B Budhwar Peth, Appa Balwant Chowk
Pune 411 002
email: ncbapune@ncbapvtltd.com

GSS Shopping Complex, 1st Floor
Opposite College Post Office, Convent Road
Ernakulam 682 035
email: ncbaernk@ncbapvtltd.com

Shop No. 15, Bharati Towers, Ground Floor
Forest Park, **Bhubaneswar** 751 001
email: ncbabub@ncbapvtltd.com

First Edition, October 2011, India

ISBN: 81-7819-083-4

Design and type setting at

Write Wing Advertising, Kolkata

Consulting Editor: Barnali Roy

Art direction & illustrations : Joydip Routh
Photography: Debasish Sen

Printed at: RB Lamination, Kolkata

Price: ₹ 499.00

Disclaimer

In this book you will find many interesting and authentic recipes and
house-hold tips which you may like to try out. Though, we are sure
this are all tried and tested, as a matter of form must inform you that as the publisher,
will not be held responsible for any damages or loss, property-wise or health-wise,
that you may incur during experimentation.

For Rohan

Acknowledgements

Mohua Mitra	Barnali Roy
Nandinee Pal	Debi Sen
Tom Roychowdhury	Sudeshna Banerjee
Jonaki Mitra	Madhuri Gupta
Himani Sen	Puspalata Routh
Arijit Sengupta	Radharani Mitra
Hiralal Seal	Shukla Mitra
Indrani Sen	Supriya Ray
Kalyan De	Dipika Sen
Kushal Mookherjee	Padma Mazumdar

Contents

Contents

Preface

Harir Khobor, the magazines from which this book has been sourced, had become popular beyond all expectations.

In 1999 Debasish, my colleagues and I produced Kolkata's first quarterly Bengali food magazine called *Harir Khobor*. The title is a Bengali phrase with a double entendre, translated, it means 'news from the cauldron' – a tongue-in-cheek expression for hot gossip!

As far as I am aware, no other Bengali food magazine existed then or even now. The motivation being that most of my colleagues are dedicated foodies. When we are not planning and executing advertising campaigns for food products or beverages, our thoughts invariably turn to food. The prospect of a food journal was delicious!

Animated discussions in the office about treasured recipes handed down by mothers or grandmothers, nostalgic food memories and culinary experiences were shared. Indeed, food was uppermost in our minds, in between client meetings, brainstorms and presentations. Occasionally, these office chit-chats led to experiments. The recipes were noted for future use.

Many keen readers contributed recipes, culinary tales, views and food history. We had the privilege of interviewing well known personalities and legendary epicureans. From the large and miscellaneous collection we selected articles and recipes related to Bengal. Perhaps in the future we may be able to bring a sequel based on various other culinary delights from India and the world.

There was yet another reason why *Harir Khobor* was launched. This was a personal one. Thoughts of food inevitably evoke happy memories and it is certainly no different with me. Food takes me back to my childhood days and to our kitchen in my family home on Rowland Road, Kolkata.

I remember so well our table laden with steaming, hot, delicately spiced and fragrant dishes at mealtimes. Each dish planned meticulously by my mother to tempt our childish, fussy appetites. While eating seasonal foods may be a modern concept worldwide, eating season's fresh pickings then almost fifty years ago came naturally to our predecessors. As every new season in Bengal yielded a brand new set of succulent, nutritious ingredients, just harvested from the fields, ponds and rivers, they formed the basis of menus and dishes that arrived at our table deliciously cooked. Every occasion had a suitable menu and every festival was observed with gastronomical passion and dedication.

I still recall vividly the repertoire of Bengali dishes made at home. My mother was the Goddess of the kitchen who planned what her immediate (and extended) family would eat – when, where and how. The cook or *baburchi* was given instructions, she only stepped into the kitchen in times of grave necessity or out of sheer love for the person she intended to please, whether a child or a relative. She was also the mistress of the cutting board or *bonti*. Her daily task was to plan the menu, check the vegetable baskets and select the best vegetables, then peel, chop and cut them into the proper shapes befitting the recipe, thereby adding her personal and loving touch to every dish without ever having to slave over a hot stove!

Unfortunately, these recipes were handed down by word-of-mouth and no written record remains. Perhaps the art of cooking in those days did not depend so much on fine measurements and structured methods, but on creative judgment. This book then, is a loving tribute to the woman who taught me just why and how eating can be one of life's great pleasures, and equally, a concrete, written testament and reminder to the next, scattered, *probashi* or immigrant generation about Bengal and our rich culinary heritage.

Perhaps one day my grandson Rohan and his children may wish to rediscover their culinary heritage. Then, all they have to do, is simply turn the pages of this book.

Introduction _____

"And I think very fondly of food
Though I'm broody at time
When bothered by rhymes
I brood.
On food"

— Ogden Nash

Harir Khobor attempts to bring the reader a comprehensive guide to quintessential Bengali food fare and culture. This volume is a collection of remembered thoughts woven together with tried and trusted recipes. The sub title of the book "What's Cooking in Bengal" should be taken in the sense that we are talking of Bengali food only!

The book is beamed at a wider audience and targeted to the younger generation of Indians here and abroad. With the hope that those who have roots in Bengal, may discover Bengal through its food and customs.

The chapters unfold sequentially. A Bengali meal is served and enjoyed in an orderly sequence. Like Indian classical music, a meal starts with an overture or *'alaap'*, establishing the theme or *'raag'* corresponding to the season. The somewhat unfussy beginnings lead to the middle, comprising seasonal vegetarian variations which then unfolds the main course which would be the season's choicest non-vegetarian items. The finale is announced with a mélange of sweet and piquant chutneys. The meal ends with a flourish and a choice of rich desserts. The accompaniments are usually rice or puffy light *luchis* or pancakes. In this book the chapters take the reader through a similar sequence. Each section begins with an introduction.

As everywhere else in the world food reflects the culture and history of its region. In the last three hundred years, Bengal has had to withstand foreign invasions and colonization. But has managed to weave alien influences and retain its own traditions. Bengal was ruled not only by Hindu chiefs and kings, but by Muslim, Portuguese, Dutch and British rulers as well. Thus a complex culture and food habits emerged, weaving religious and ethnic traditions to what was an inherently rustic diet. Much of the Bengali preparations have peasant origins. The recipes have survived through verbal communications.

A refreshing aspect of Bengali cuisine, is its dependence on the seasons. Cold storages and super markets are recent innovations. Bengalis, even now largely depend on farm fresh products. Everyone believes in eating what is in season, because Nature knows best! In the book, you will find chapters that tell of seasonal products and recipes. Then again these traditions are linked to festivals and religious occasions. We have given brief descriptions of these age old customs of Pujas, as well as weddings and other rituals and their corresponding culinary essentials.

"Waste not, want not" is the credo of most Bengali kitchens. Bengal was devastated by a famine in the early forties. Villagers survived on meagre gleanings from fields and ponds. Satyajit Ray, the famous film director, captures the deprivation in his films *"Pather Panchali"* and *"Ashani Sanket"*. Perhaps, memory lingers of those dark days, wastage is not tolerated easily. Shoots, stems, leaves and even flowers are carefully saved relished here, thrift rules! The *"Charchchari"* and "Fries" chapters, showcase a few recipes on leftovers.

But not all Bengali cooking is about thrift and chewing roots and shoots! In the early 20th century, rich traders and merchants began to prosper under British patronage. It was the age of intellectual renaissance, art and culture flourished in Kolkata's elite social circles. Abundance of wealth was reflected in their lavish lifestyles. The Tagores of Jorasanko, Rabindra Nath Tagore's family, were noted for their wealth and culture. Their palatial family home was renowned for its grand architecture, multitude of servants, carriages, chandeliers, soirees and great hospitality. The refined ladies of the house orchestrated the running of the kitchens. We had the privilege of talking to a descendant of the Tagore family and bring you snippets of their culinary preferences.

Mr R P Gupta, a well known public figure, a bibliophile, avid collector, scholar, gastronomic writer had spoken at length about Calcutta food in the 50's to *Harir Khobor*. The interview was published in the magazine. The late R P Gupta was well known for his love of the arts and finer things of life. Food was his passion. He had remarked that the Bengalis' insatiable appetite for food would reduce them to paupers," they exhaust all their money on food". He said, "eating was a group activity in Calcutta, has been and always will be." From his reminiscences a graphic picture emerges a glimpse of 'café' culture and food of his times.

As an editor, I had to pick and choose the articles and recipes from a vast collection. The chapter on "Tea" is a reflection of a young reader's thoughts. "Cook by Fluke" is a first hand experience of the writer. The articles were chosen for their simplicity and easy recipes. Much of it, specially the chapter on picnics and Darjeeling, as well as some others are personal memories. The book is a memoir of food as well as a miscellany of Bengali recipes.

The book is largely a collective enterprise and translated from Bengali.

Special thanks must be given to Debasish Sen, print expert, foodie, cook, wildlife enthusiast and a keen photographer. To Joydip Routh, Creative Chief, for his wonderful illustrations and layouts. Sandipan Saha for helping with mechanical details and Somnath Gain for setting the text.

I thank Barnali Roy for her interest and advice. My daughter Debi Sen for correcting my awful prose by e-mail. My husband Prodosh Sen for his support and encouragement. I thank the team for hands on cooking, experimenting, tasting and putting it all together. All for the love of Bengali food.

Bhaat

Bhaater Hari

– the rice pot

"Aay brishti jhepe, dhaan debo mepe..." *

— Bengali folk song

Last Sunday, I was invited to my childhood friend Subroto's house for lunch. While we were talking, *Mashima*, Subroto's mother, entered the room and said,

"lunch is almost ready, the rice is being boiled."

She seemed like Goddess *Annapurna* (the rice giving Goddess of Bengal) standing before us to assuage our hunger. The aroma of boiling rice filled the house and all at once I began to feel ravenous. Soon we sat down to a meal cooked to perfection, but what attracted my eyes first, was not the beautifully arranged little silver bowls or *'baatis'* of fragrant yellow, oil-beaded fish and chicken curries, nor the aromatic and lightly spiced vegetables or mounds of crisp fried vegetable peel starters but the gleaming mound of fresh cooked rice, each grain a fluffy ode to flawlessness, a promise soon turned into reality with the first heavenly mouthful.

And that, in a nutshell, is the very foundation of every good Bengali meal – the rice. Essential, life giving, soothing in times of illnesses, the ultimate comfort food, the ideal foil to any other Bengali dish and part of the very fabric of Bengali life.

The Bengali has always been called *'bheto'*, or one who subsists on rice (*'bhaat'* being the Bengali word for cooked rice). Why is a Bengali so partial to rice or *'bhaat'*? Bengalis say "if I don't work hard, where will my *'bhaat'* come from?" or the penniless laments, "today the rice pot did not touch the stove". When things are easy it is said "oh it's as simple as *jal-bhaat*". During illness, when a fever rages, Bengalis shun rice. A myth perhaps but rice is

* *"Rain, pour forth with might, and I'll give you a measure-full of rice..."*

considered to make body temperatures rise. Thus the way to find out if a person has recuperated is to politely enquire, "Have you had *'bhaat'* today?" In other words if a Bengali has had his rice, he is on the road to recovery. And yet, for stomach upsets, soft rice and stews are permitted. Only rice soothes and satisfies.

In other words *'bhaat'* is the soul of Bengal's psyche. Not surprising, because rice grows easily in the state of Bengal. The land is rich and fertile. The weather is conducive. Rice is nature's golden gift to Bengal. The mention of rice is found in many historical and religious texts. It was the main offering at *'pujas'* and rituals, as it is even today. From pre-Buddhist days rice became the staple of Bengal. One finds references to *'pulandu'* (pilaus) and *'yagnas'* that required rice. Later after the reign of the Hindu kings, the Muslim rulers introduced Bengal to Biriyanis, but many types of rice and its variants – puffed, roasted, boiled and flattened continue to be an integral part of the Bengali diet.

——— VARIETIES OF RICE ———

Buying rice can be bewildering – to be confronted by a dizzying array of varieties with different names... *'Chamarmani'*, *'Dudher shar'* ('milk cream' in Bengali), *'Basmati'*, *'Dehradun'*, *'Gobindobhog'*, *'Kaminibhog'*, *'Golapsarup'*, *'Pahari aatap'* are a few descriptive names. Which one to buy? Which to eat every day? Which is more nutritious? Which kind is best for pilaus and parties? Who would have thought that the starchy carbohydrate could come in so many varieties!

Here are some of our pickings. Fine long rice is recommended for pilaus. Seed-like aromatic *'Gobindobhog'*, has the aroma of flowers. It is light and good as a daily staple. It is also perfect for making rice puddings. Brown, coarse rice tastes best with hot fish and vegetable curries. It is par boiled, keeps the vitamins sealed. It is the most nutritious, inexpensive and the common man's choice.

As for something more exotic, one has to look further afield for these more unusual strains of locally grown rice. *Bonolakshmi* farm in Bolpur, grows a variety of rice named *'Randhuni-pagol'* ('one that drives a cook crazy'). This variety, they say, fills the house with a tantalizing and maddeningly rich aroma! Trust the Bengalis to wax poetic about rice! *Bonolakshmi* farm grows two other special types of par-boiled rice, the *'Banshkathi'* and *'Kabiraj-shal'*. Both are delicious and best eaten with home cooked simple vegetable dishes.

At Raigunj in Dinajpur district, one can sample the *'Tula-penja'* ('cottonwool'), rice that on cooking is said to become as soft and fluffy. The famous rice of Jalpaiguri, another district in north Bengal, is the 'Kalo Nunia' ('black salted'), eaten both as parboiled and white rice.

Red or brown rice is unpolished rice, they retain the nutrients within each grain. Red rice is popular in Bangladesh. It is delicious with dried fish and hot curries.

The most royal of all is Basmati which grows in the undulating plains of north India. This world-renowned rice is long grained, fragrant and the essential requisite for exotic Biriyanis and pilaus. This type of rice is not an everyday choice for most Bengalis.

─────── RICE & RITES ───────

Rice is inextricably woven into the fabric of Bengali rituals. In olden days it was vital to have a well stocked store, where drums or sacks of rice were kept for the whole year. If nothing else a Bengali could survive on boiled rice, salt and a few greens. As for a feast, it is incomplete and shocking if there is no rice or 'polau' in the menu. It is not surprising that in rituals of birth, marriage or death rice plays a justifiably important role.

The first auspicious ceremony for a child is 'Mukhe bhaat', or 'Annaprashan', The baby's fed the first spoon of cooked rice by the maternal uncle. Henceforth, rice will be the cereal, the child will grow up on and come to enjoy. In keeping with the significance of the ceremony it is customary for the parents to invite guests to a feast afterwards.

Much later as the children grow up and get married, rice is still given its due respect. Rice or puffed rice is showered on the ritual fire by the couple as a symbolic offering. At the pre wedding rite called 'Aay buro bhaat' or pre-nuptial rice, the groom and bride-to-be celebrate their last days of bachelorhood in individual homes with a grand feast for friends and family. (Read more about it in Bengali Ceremonies and Cuisine).

Before a bride sets off for her new home, she pays off her debt to her parents by giving back some rice, a symbolic gesture of gratitude. Can one be grateful for anything else?

In the lives of Bengalis rice plays a multi-faceted, exalted role. In everyday conversation, one may be asked, 'Have you had rice'? It really means have you had a proper meal? No wonder the new husband promises to take lifelong care of his wife by presenting her with 'Bhaat-kapor' (food and clothes).

Even birthdays are celebrated with 'Payesh' or 'Paramanno' a creamy rice pudding, with a prayer and hope for long life. In death rice is indispensable. The departed soul is offered a 'Pindadan' made of rice.

--------- RECIPES ---------

Bhaate-e-bhaat (boiled rice and vegetables)

When there is a hurry, and no time to cook an elaborate meal *'bhaatey'* is the solution. What is a *'bhaatey'*? It is simply a pot of boiling rice with assorted vegetables thrown in. The vegetables are mashed with butter of ghee (clarified butter) and salt, eaten with the boiled rice. So what's so special about it?

It makes a quick and fortifying breakfast. In the olden days of the joint family, womenfolk could not cater to different tastes and needs of family and children so early in the day. They had to go to schools or offices more or less at the same time. In this mad rush of getting ready, packing school bags and making tiffins, where was the time to feed so many? Thus was born the easy and convenient rice porridge. Boring? Not at all. In fact with imagination and innovations, the *bhaatey* can turn into a delicious treat. The vegetables need to be chosen carefully, each variety ought to be boiled separately (not with the rice like in the olden days), peeled then served with hot and spicy pickles, pungent mustard oil and other piquant condiments. Each person dresses the vegetables according his or her choice. Therein lies the art of *bhatey* – its 'do it your way'!

Method:

'Bhaate' is any vegetable – potato, red pumpkin, brinjal, okra, or whatever fresh vegetable is in season – boiled whole, often in the same pot in which rice is being cooked, then mashed and flavoured with a sprinkling of salt, a drizzle of mustard oil, mustard sauce (*Kasundi*), chopped onions and green chillies. It is eaten with the rice, sometimes with a spoon of ghee. Boiled eggs can also be added for a protein boost.

Phaney Bhaat (rice with starch)

'Phaney Bhaat' can be cooked together with any aromatic rice (*Gobindobhog* or *Basmati* etc.) with seasonal vegetables (potato, red pumpkin, brinjal, okra, parval etc.), boiled whole or diced, without draining the starch. It is eaten with a sprinkling of salt, ghee or butter and green chllies.

Tips
Salt melts fast in the monsoons. To keep salt dry, put a small cloth bag of rice in the salt container, to prevent the salt from melting.

Paanta Bhaat (fermented rice)

This is peasant fare and a welcome change for city dwellers in hot weather. In the old days, rice would be cooked for the entire family in a huge pot. If all was not consumed, the leftover rice was not what a parsimonious Bengali was going to throw out. There were no refrigerators then. In many villages there are none even now. The rice was steeped in water overnight instead. This slightly fermented rice was eaten the next day along with the water.

Though some might turn up their noses at this dish, terming it as fit only for villagers, it can be delicious when teamed with the right accompaniments.

Method:

Boil rice, drain the starch and soak in water overnight. It can be refrigerated.

At lunch the next day, the rice is eaten with a squeeze of lime, chopped onions and green chillies. The water is cooling and delicious. For a spicier version, add roasted red chillies and fried garlic. Then there are the add-ons of fried balls of poppy seed, lentils or shrimps, together this cooling summer fare is filling and delicious.

Pish Pash (rice and chicken khichuri)

Serves four

Ingredients:

| Rice – 250 gms (washed and clean) |
| Chicken – 500 gms (cut into pieces) |
| White oil – 2 tbsp |
| Carrot – 2 large (chopped in cubes) |
| Bean – 100 gms (cut into 2"pcs) |
| Ripe Tomato –2 (cubed) |
| Potato – 4 (cubed) |
| Ginger – 2" stem (finely chopped) |
| Onion – 2 large (finely chopped) |
| Bay leaf – 2 |
| Cinnamon stick – 2 (1" pcs) |
| Green cardamom pod – 3 |
| Black peppercorn – 1 tsp (whole) |
| Clove – 3 |
| Butter – 25 gms (to serve) |
| Salt & sugar – to taste |

Method:

Boil chicken pieces with a little salt. Keep chicken and stock aside. Remove scum from stock.

In a deep pan, heat oil and fry bay leaves, cinnamon, cloves, cardamom, peppercorns, ginger and onions. Fry till they are transparent. Then put in the rice, stir for a while. Add the chicken stock, strain to remove all scum. Add potatoes and carrots. When rice starts to boil and the vegetables are tender put in the previously boiled chicken. It is a one pot dish. Serve hot, topped with butter.

Ghee Bhaat (bengali pilau)

Serves six

Ingredients:

Basmati rice – 500 gms

Ghee or oil for a low fat version – 150 gm

Cashew nut – 50 gms & raisin – 20 gms

Onion – 200 gms (sliced & fried)

Bay leaf & clove – 4

Green cardamom – 6

Cinnamon – 2 inches & saffron – a pinch

Warm water – 4 cups

Salt & sugar – to taste

• You can also add frozen or fresh green peas

Method:

Soak rice in water for 30 minutes, wash, drain and dry. Heat ghee, fry cashew and raisins lightly, remove and keep aside. Add bay leaves, green cardamom, cloves, cinnamon and fry. Add rice and sugar, stir for a minute. Add warm water and bring to boil, cook until half done. Add the fried cashews and raisins, mix well. Cover the pan with a tight lid, cook on low heat till done. Sprinkle ghee and fried onions (optional) before serving.

Maangsho Bhaat (meat pilau)

Serves six

Ingredients:

Meat/ mutton – 500 gms

Basmati rice – 500 gms

Ghee or oil for a low fat version – 200 gms

Yoghurt – 200 gms

Onion – 4 tbsp (paste)

Onion – 250 gms (sliced)

Ginger paste – 2 tbsp & garlic paste – 2 tsp

Bay leaf – 4

Black cumin seed (*Shah jeera*) – 1tsp

Special *garam masala* powder - 2 tbsp

Salt – to taste

Special Garam Masala powder:
green cardamom - 6 , black cardamom – 4, nutmeg -1, cinnamon - 2" stick, clove - 6, dried red chilli - 2, mace -1 and black cumin seed (*shah jeera*) - 1 teaspoon. Roast these items together and grind to a powder.

Method:

Marinate meat pieces with turmeric, salt, half of the Special *garam masala* powder, onion, ginger and garlic pastes, yoghurt and marinate for 2 hours. Soak rice in water for 15 minutes, wash, drain and spread out to dry. Simmer marinated meat, till almost done. Take out meat pieces from the water and stir fry. Keep stock aside.

Heat 100 gms ghee or oil in a pan, fry onions till golden brown, remove and keep aside. Add more ghee to the pan, and bay leaves, black cumin seeds and fry till it releases an aroma. Then add dried rice, stir fry for 3-4 minutes. Add meat pieces, pour the stock, bring to boil, cover the pan with a tight lid, cook in slow fire till done. Sprinkle fried onions and special *garam masala* powder before serving.

Illish Machher Polau (hilsa pilau) | Serves four

Ingredients:

Basmati rice – 400 gms
Hilsa – 8 pieces
Sunflower oil – 100 gms
Ghee – 50 gms
Cashew nut – 50 gms
Raisin – 20 gms
Bay leaf – 4
Green cardamom – 4
Clove – 4
Green chilli – 4 (slit & seeded)
Warm water – 4 cups
Salt & sugar – to taste

Method:

Soak rice in water for 30 minutes, wash, drain and spread to dry. Heat oil in a pan, fry hilsa pieces very lightly, remove and keep aside. In the same oil put cashew, raisins, cardamom and cloves fry lightly, then add bay leaves, rice, sugar and a little salt. Stir-fry for a minute. Add warm water, cook until half done. Take a heavy pan and arrange rice and fried hilsa pieces in layers, top with green chillies and ghee, sprinkle water. Cover the pan tightly, seal the edges. Cook for 10 minutes in medium heat. Remove from fire, serve hot.

Lebu Bhaat (lemon rice) | Serves four

Ingredients:

Basmati rice – 400 gms
Ginger paste – 1 ½ tbsp
Green pea – 250 gms
Sunflower oil – 100 gms
Raisin – 20 gms
Lemon leaf – 4
Clove & cardamom – 4 (whole)
Cinnamon – 2 stick (one inch each)
Mustard seed – 2 tsp
Green chilli – 4 (slit & seeded)
Warm water – 4 cups
Salt & sugar – to taste

Method:

Wash peas and keep aside. Rinse rice in water, drain and spread to dry. Heat oil in a pan (keep aside 1 tbsp for tempering) fry raisins, cardamom, cloves lightly, then add green peas, ginger paste, rice, sugar and a little salt. Stir-fry for a minute. Add warm water and lemon leaves, cook until done. Heat rest of the oil in a pan sprinkle mustard seeds fry till they splutter, now add cooked rice carefully, mix well. Cover the pan with a lid, cook in low heat for 2-3 minutes. Remove from fire. Serve hot.

Teto

Shurute Teto

— bitter start

"I will let loose against you the fleet- footed vines
I will call in the jungle to stamp out your lines
The roofs shall fade before it
The house-beams shall fall:
And the karela, the bitter karela, shall cover it all!"
— Rudyard Kipling

Not surprising that *'karela'* is not the most popular of vegetables. It's lunch-time in Kolkata on a Sunday in May, the temperature outside is around 42° Celsius, cuckoos are calling and the sun is a burning disc upon a cloudless sky. It's summer with a vengeance and time for a suitably light, easily digestible and cooling lunch for the family before the ritual of the afternoon siesta. The family is seated around the dining table – eight-year-old Srijoyee, her parents, grandmother, uncle and older sister. The food on the table is abundant and suited to the season. There's brinjal fried with *neem* leaves, ridge gourd cooked with poppy seeds, fish gravy with tender parvals, lentils to which raw mango was added and a tart dish of tiny, fresh-water fish.

But Srijoyee doesn't like everything on the menu. One mouthful of the brinjal and she starts to fuss. Her mother, not wanting to ruin the only holiday in her week, quickly gives Srijoyee a dollop of tomato ketchup to take away the bitter taste. But this annoys 'dida', grandmother: after all, not only does the bitter flavour act as an appetiser, but she knows that eating bitter food in the summer is the best way to stay healthy.

Perhaps the tradition of starting a meal with something bitter and ending it with something sweet-sour is about to disappear. People seem to be too busy to cook and eat a proper lunch. But should we ignore the scientific background to the rules governing our traditional cooking and eating habits? Certainly not without losing a part of our rich heritage and a wealth of ancient wisdom that could be just the key to keeping us all healthy. After all, a good digestion, say experts, is the foundation of good health and long life.

Bengali cuisine is Ayurvedic – the menu includes a complete range of tastes: bitter, salty, hot, sour and sweet, all of which are needed for good health. Bitter food is most beneficial to counteract the heat of summer. *Neem* leaves, bitter gourd, *kalmegh*

(a bitter medicinal plant) and the leaves of *shewli* (a plant known for its fragrant white flowers) are all good for the liver. *Neem* also cures several diseases of the skin and stomach. Eating bitter gourd kills intestinal worms and prevents acidity, and drinking its raw juice reduces blood sugar. The bitter leaves of the parval (*paltaa paata*) are a natural source of digestive powers.

Serving food the Bengali way is an art. There are rules to follow, almost like classical music. We start with the *aalaap* and then progress one step at a time. Towards the end we reach the sour food, then change taste again to reach the sweet. The meal starts with bitter food, but the skill that goes into cooking makes the bitter wonderfully palatable.

🍂 *Neem* 🍂

Neem — *Azadirachta indica* is a tree in the mahogany family **Meliaceae**, and is native to Indian Subcontinent, growing in tropical and semi-tropical regions. *Neem* is a fast-growing tree that can reach a height of 15–20 m (about 50–65 feet), rarely to 35–40 m (115–131 feet).

- In India, the tree is variously known as "Sacred Tree," "Heal All," "Nature's Drugstore," "Village Pharmacy" and "Panacea for all diseases." All parts of the tree are said to have medicinal properties (seeds, leaves, flowers and bark) and are used for preparing many different medical preparations and is useful for skin care.

- Hanging a bunch of *Neem* leaves above the kitchen door. keeps flies away. *Neem* leaves are an effective and natural insect repellant.

——— RECIPES ———

Neem Begun Bhaaja (brinjal fried with *neem* leaves)
Serves four

Ingredients:

Neem leaf (tender) – a handful

Brinjal – 250 gms

Turmeric powder/ paste – ½ tsp

Mustard oil – 1 tbsp

Salt – to taste

Method:

Wash and dry the *neem* leaves. Cut the brinjal into small pieces and smear with turmeric and salt.

In hot oil, fry *neem* leaves till they are crisp. Remove the leaves and keep aside. In the same oil, fry the brinjal pieces till they are soft, then blend in the *neem* leaves.

- This is eaten with rice at lunch, particularly in summer.

——— 🎐 ———

Neem Jhol (mixed vegetables with *neem* leaves)
Serves six

Ingredients:

Neem leaf (tender) – 8 to 10

Brinjal – 200 gms

Ridge gourd – 200 gms

Raw banana – 1

Green papaya – 200 gms

Sweet potato – 200 gms

Broad bean – 150 gms

Turmeric powder/ paste – ½ tsp

Mustard oil – 1 tbsp

Mustard seed – ½ tsp

Fenugreek seed – ½ tsp

Coriander powder/ paste – 1½ tsp

Ginger paste – 1½ tsp

Salt – to taste

Method:

Chop all the vegetables. Smear the brinjal and raw banana pieces with turmeric.

Fry the mustard and fenugreek seeds in hot oil. Then add the vegetables and fry for a few minutes.

Blend in the pastes then add water and salt. Cover and cook till the vegetables are done.

Lastly add the *neem* leaves and simmer little longer. Let it cool before serving.

- Bitter food is usually served in small portions at the beginning of the meal, so you will need a lesser quantity of vegetables than usual.
- This item is eaten cold.
- It should taste fairly bitter.

Paltar Bora (parval leaf fritters)
Serves four

Ingredients:

Dried pea lentil – 200 gms

Parval leaf – A bunch (chopped)

Mustard oil – 100 gms

Green chilli – 2 (chopped fine)

Salt – to taste

Method:

Soak the lentils. Grind, make a thick paste. Mix in the parval leaves, salt and green chillies. Form balls, deep fry until brown and crisp.

Uchchhe Charchchari (dry mixed vegetables with bitter gourd)
Serves four

Ingredients:

Bitter gourd – 200 gms

Potato – 200 gms

Drumstick – 2 to 3 sticks

Brinjal – 200 gms

Mustard oil – 1 tbsp

Dried lentil ball (bori) – 8

Panch phoron – 1 tsp

Ginger paste – 1 ½ tsp

Salt – to taste

Method:

Dice all vegetables. Fry the *bories* and keep aside. Add *panch phoron* to the oil and then add the vegetables. Fry for several minutes.

Add salt, *bori* and water, cover and cook.

When the vegetables are done and the water has been absorbed, blend in the ginger, fry for a minute and remove from fire.

Chingri Diye Uchchhe Charchchari (bitter gourd with shrimps)
Serves four

Ingredients:

Shrimp – ¾ cup

Bitter gourd – 150 gms

Potato – 250 gms

Onion – 200 gms (chopped)

Mustard oil – 125 gms

Panch phoron – ½ tsp

Red chilli powder/ paste – 2 tsp

Salt – to taste

Method:

Slice the potatoes in rounds and parboil. Quarter the bitter gourds and smear with turmeric. Heat oil, fry *panch phoron* lightly. Add the bitter gourds, onions, red chillies and shrimps, in stages, stir fry. Add the potatoes and fry some more. Season, cover and cook, sprinkle water from time to time, if needed.

- Brinjals can also be included with the potatoes.

——— SHUKTO BASICS ———

There are several types of *shukto*. If it's bitter, it is necessary to use bitter gourd/ *neem* leaves, but for ordinary '*shukto*' made with gourd or parval, bitters are not required. *Shukto* may be made with red *shaak* or shrimps. What characterises '*shukto*' is the combination of ginger, milk and the fried spices—mustard, fenugreek or *randhuni** seeds.

* Seeds of Indian Parsley

Traditional Shukto (mixed vegetable curry with bitter gourd) | Serves four

Ingredients:

Bitter gourd – 100 gms

Sweet potato – 150 gms

Mustard oil – 1½ tbsp

Dried lentil ball *(Bori)* – 25 gms

Coriander powder/ paste – 1 tsp

Mustard paste – 1 tbsp

Mustard seed(whole) – ¼ tsp

Randhuni seed (whole)– ¼ tsp

Bay leaf –2

Potato – 150 gms

Drumstick – 4 sticks

Brinjal – 150 gms

Raw banana – 1

Ginger paste – ½ tbsp

Milk – ½ cup

Randhuni paste – ½ tsp

Salt & sugar – to taste

Method:

Scrape bitter gourds and cut them into 12-14 pieces. Cut the rest of the vegetables into thin strips.

Fry the *boris* until crisp and keep aside.

In the same oil, fry the bitter gourd pieces, potatoes for a few minutes. Then add salt, coriander and mustard paste, pour water. When it comes to a boil, add remaining vegetables, cover and cook. After vegetables are done, add *boris* and cook till they are soft.

Heat oil in a fresh pan and fry the bay leaves, mustard and *randhuni* seeds till they crackle; next add the ginger paste. Fry for a few minutes. Pour vegetable stew into this. Add salt, sugar, *randhuni* paste and milk, to the pan.

Bring to a boil before removing from fire. Serve cooled.

- For a change of taste, use different combinations of spices – mustard and fenugreek seeds or mustard, fenugreek with *randhuni* seeds.

- Add aniseed/ fennel powder *(mouri)* for a different flavour.

Mourala Machher Shukto (mixed vegetable curry with sprats) | Serves six

Ingredients:

Mola carplet/ white bait – 300 gms

Potato – 200 gms

Brinjal – 200 gms

Red pumpkin – 150 gms

Broad bean – 100 gms

Raw banana – 1 (large)

Sweet potato – 150 gms

Fenugreek seed – 1 tsp

Ginger paste – 1½ tsp

Mustard paste – 2 ½ tbsp

Mustard oil – 50 gms

Turmeric powder/ paste – ½ tsp

Salt – to taste

Method:

De-scale, clean and wash fish thoroughly. Smear with turmeric and salt. Heat half of the oil in a wok and fry fish lightly and keep aside.

Wash, peel and cut vegetables length wise. Heat rest of the oil and then add fenugreek seeds and all vegetables. Stir fry for 3 to 4 minutes. Pour a cup of water, salt and cook till vegetables are tender, add fried fish. Next, mix mustard and ginger pastes with water in a bowl, stir well and pour over the vegetable stew, simmer for a few minutes and remove from fire.

Machh Diye Uchchhe Charchchari (stir fried bitter gourd with fish)

Ingredients:

Rahu/ Katla fish – 300 gms (large pieces)

Bitter gourd – 150 gms

Potato – 200 gms

Red pumpkin – 150 gms

Mustard seed – 1 tsp

Dried red chilli – 2 (whole)

Ginger paste – 1 ½ tsp

Turmeric powder/ paste – 1 tsp

Mustard oil – 50 gms

Salt – to taste

Method:

| Serves four

Wash, peel and cut potatoes lengthwise. Similarly cut bitter gourds and red pumpkin. Smear the fish pieces with turmeric and salt, fry well in half of the oil, remove, de-bone, break into flakes and keep aside. Heat rest of the oil and then temper with mustard seeds and dried red chillies, stir till brown, add all the vegetables then fry for 3 to 4 minutes, mix ginger paste, fry for another 2 minutes. Add fish flakes and salt, sprinkle water, cover and cook till done.

Teto Daal Option I (red lentils with bitter gourd)

Ingredients:

Red lentil *(mushur daal)* – 250 gms

Bitter gourd – 150 gms

Mustard oil – 1½ tbsp

Turmeric powder/ paste – ½ tsp

Dried red chilli –1 (whole)

Mustard seed – ½ tsp

Ginger – 2 half-inch pieces (shredded)

Salt – to taste

Method:

Boil the lentils. Cut the bitter gourds and fry lightly in oil. Add these, with turmeric and salt to the *daal*. Temper the *daal* with whole red chilli, mustard seeds and ginger.

• The recipe should taste slightly bitter.

• *Kancha mooger daal* is another option.

Teto Daal Option II (split dried peas with bitter gourd)

Ingredients:

Dried pea lentil – 250 gms

Bitter gourd – 100 gms

Ridge gourd – 200 gms

Brinjal – 200 gms

Broad bean – 100 gms

Turmeric powder/ paste – ½ tsp

Mustard oil – 1 tbsp

Fenugreek seed – ½ tsp

Dried red chilli – 2 (whole)

Ginger paste – 1 tsp

Randhuni paste – 1 tsp

Ghee – 1½ tsp

Salt – to taste

Method:

Boil the lentils. Cut the vegetables into large pieces, add to the *daal* along with the turmeric and salt and cook till done.

Season the lentils with the fenugreek seeds and red chillies.

Add the ginger and *randhuni* pastes, and top with ghee.

Shaak

Savouring Shaak

– leafy greens

Spinach or *shaak* (a generic Bengali term that encompasses all leafy greens) is a very humdrum, easy-to-grow vegetable. *Shaak* is an essential accompaniment to rice and *daal*. Hundreds of varieties of spinach grow in the fields and vegetable patches of Bengal. Early morning dewy-fresh pickings are the best. Fresh green spinach shoots or tendrils escaping from overloaded cane baskets or bundled up carelessly on vegetable stands in the bazaars are a common sight in Kolkata on wet monsoon mornings.

Countless varieties of edible spinach grace the tables of Bengali homes. The most sought-after in winter is the *paalang* (spinach). Monsoon is the ideal season for other varieties of lush, leafy greens. Shoots, stalks and even the roots of these greens are edible and used to cook up tasty dishes to add zest to a wet day.

Monsoon brings forth the *pui* and *kalmi shaak*. *Kochu shaak* comprises the large leaves and stalks of yam/ taro plants. *Kumro* and *lau shaak* (the leaves and stalks of the pumpkin and gourd) are backyard vegetables that are devoured with relish. The red spinach is a popular variety and is often eaten fried with *kasundi*, a tangy and pungent mustard paste. In winter, mustard greens appear. Picked just before the mustard seeds ripen, these greens have a sharp flavour. Even the radish leaves and stalks are considered *shaak* varieties. So are the aromatic leaves of *methi* (fenugreek greens). The *daata* and *notey shaak* grow effortlessly in muddy tracts and are a favourite of the not-so-well-off for a nourishing meal that uses every bit of the entire plant.

Bengali seeks the unusual varieties of shaak. Some of these are not cultivated commercially. Lesser-known delicious and sometimes efficacious varieties (many varieties are remedies for illnesses), of which a few species may fall into the category of herbs have to be procured with the help of a friendly farmer! Even the leaves of marigold flowers are eaten. The fiddle sticks or curled heads of ferns are also much sought-after. *Palta* are the leaves of tender *potol* or parval. They are somewhat bitter, but good for one's health. The *sajney* is a tall tree, which has white blossoms (very edible) and long pulpy pods enriched with vitamin C. And then there's the ordinary green pea leaves and shoots or *mator shaak*, the tender ones picked in winter, make a delicious fry.

Even during religious festivals and celebrations, the seemingly humble *shaak* has a role to play. For instance, during Kali puja it is customary to eat fourteen species of *shaak* to ward off evil spirits. This goes to show that fourteen types of *shaaks* grow simultaneously during the end of the monsoon, just at the time of the puja festivals, when the earth appears to burst forth in a riot of fecundity and richness. On the last day of the Durga puja, the Goddess is propitiated with tender, fresh, juicy *kochu shaak*.

Why do Bengalis enjoy their *shaak* or spinach so much? Because, from childhood, Bengalis are taught to enjoy their greens. Above all, Bengali leafy greens are easy to cook, delicious, versatile and full of fibre and vitamins as well as being an inexpensive way to add flavour and taste to a meal. *Shaak* is most definitely a lunch time treat.

Kalmi shaak

Ipomoea aquatica is a semi-aquatic tropical plant grown as a leaf vegetable. It is known in English as Water Spinach, Water Morning Glory or Aquatic Greens. In Bengal it is known as *Kalmi shaak*. It is found throughout the tropical and subtropical regions, specially in East and Southeast Asia. It grows in water or on moist soil. It is also used extensively in Malay and Chinese cuisine, the leaves are usually stir fried with chilli pepper, garlic, ginger, dried shrimp paste and other spices.

—— RECIPES ——

Kochu Shaak (taro stalks)

Ingredients:

Taro stalk – 2 bundles

Mustard oil –1½ tbsp

Coconut (fresh) – 1½ cups (grated)

Panch phoron – 1 tsp

Green chilli – 2 (whole)

Flour – 1 tsp

Salt – to taste

Method:

Cut the taro stalks into 2" pieces and remove the skin. Boil and drain.

Smear a little oil on the hands (to prevent itching) and mash the boiled stalks well. Then heat most of the oil, fry the grated coconut. Heat the remaining oil, put in the *panch phoron*, then the greens and coconut with salt. Fry for 3 minutes.

Add green chillies and flour. Mix well. It should be of thick consistency.

Kalmi Shaak Bhaja (fried aquatic greens)

Ingredients:

Kalmi green – 2 bunches

Mustard oil – 1tbsp

Dried lentil ball (*bori*) – 12

Dried red chilli – 2 (whole)

Panch phoron – ½ tsp

Salt – to taste

Method:

Wash the greens thoroughly. Discard roots and chop. Fry *boris* in hot oil, remove and crush.

In the same oil, put in the spices, add the chopped greens.

Stir well and add salt. The greens will cook in their own juice.

When done sprinkle crushed *boris*.

OPTION:- It can also be tempered with fried chopped garlic.

Lal Shaak Bhaja (fried red spinach)

| Serves four

Ingredients:

Red spinach – 2 bunches

Mustard oil – 1tbsp

Dried red chilli – 2 (whole)

Onion – 1 (medium sized)

Panch phoron – ½ tsp

Salt – to taste

Method:

Discard roots and wash the red spinach thoroughly. Chop red spinach and onions finely.

Fry red chilli and *panch phoron* in hot oil, put chopped onions and fry for a minute. Add chopped red spinach, stir and fry for few minutes. Add salt and fry till dry.

Begun Diye Methi Shaak Bhaja (fried fenugreek green with brinjal)

| Serves four

Ingredients:

Fenugreek green – 2 bunches

Brinjal – 200 gms

Mustard oil – 1tbsp

Dried red chilli – 2 (whole)

Mustard seed – 1 tsp

Salt – to taste

Method:

Wash the leaves of fenugreek greens. Cut brinjal in small cubes, fry lightly and keep aside. In the same oil, fry the spices, add the leaves of fenugreek greens. Stir with salt. The leaves should cook in their own juice.

Mix fried brinjal stir for few minutes, remove from fire.

A variety of *shaak* recipes are given in the *charchchari* chapter.

Tips

- Raw bananas can leave stains, to remove the stains after cutting them, rub your hands with sour curd. Then wash your hands with soap.

- Sprinkle salt on the duster or dish cloth before wiping the dining table, this keeps flies away.

Daal

Darun Daal

– lovely lentils

"Dall roti khao, Provhu ke goon gao" *
– Popular saying

It was my daughter Debi's birthday. I have made a special lunch and set it out in a silver *thala* (plate), I arranged the small bowls of delicacies such as prawn malai curry, meat curry, vegetables and *bhajaas*, around the plate. It looked lovely and festive. The terracotta lamp flickers and rose petals are strewn on the table. A lovely aroma floats up. My daughter looks at the array of delicacies and pronounces an anticipatory 'yumm', then she frowns. 'But where is the *daal*?' she says.

Lentils are an indispensable part of a Bengali diet. They are rich in protein and a delicious prelude to lunch or dinner. *Daals* are replete with wholesome flavours and mildly spiced goodness.

The nourishing lentil stew, eaten with rice or *roti,* is the essential diet for millions not only in Bengal but the whole of India.

However, I caution the reader, the popular *daal* and *bhaat* (lentils and rice) combination is not considered complete by Bengalis, unless it is accompanied by fries. We will talk about that in the next chapter.

Innovative cooks have created clever, inventive and healthy variations on this staple, thereby rescuing it from being boring. Even the *daal* can be lifted from being humdrum and given a twist to make it worthy of a feast. Some of the variations include roasted *moog* (split green grams) cooked with fish-heads or shrimps. In winter

* *"Praise the Lord If roti and daal are all you can afford."*

the same lentil is often made with cauliflower and peas. When tempered with pure ghee and *garam masala, daal* can be divine!

The most popular and commonly used variety in Bengal is the *Mushur daal*. It is cooked to a soupy consistency, then perked up with a sprinkling of fried onion seeds or onions, or fried chopped garlic and tomatoes. Lentils such as

Arhar or *Toor* are cooked in a similar manner. In summer, *kalaier daal* (popular in the district of Burdwan) is simmered with ginger and aniseed paste to create an aromatic and soothing broth which is cooling and soothing.

The different *daals* and spices relieve the tedium on taste buds. Add seasonal vegetables into the *daal* and you have a quick and easy 'one pot' meal.

Tips

- Add a green chilli and salt to the dry mustard seeds before grinding to a paste, this prevents the mustard paste from becoming bitter.

- Add few drops of oil to the chillies to avoid the powder from blowing into your eyes and nose. This also keeps chilli powder fresh for a longer time.

- Do not throw lemons after use. Add salt and put them in a container with lid. Add a little asafoetida, sugar and chilli powder to the lemons. It makes a tasty pickle.

——— RECIPES ———

Paalang Shaak Diye Mushur Daal (red lentils with spinach) | Serves four

Ingredients:

Red lentil – 250 gms

Spinach – 200 gms (large-leaved)

Potato – 250 gms (medium)

Onion – 150 gms

Turmeric powder/ paste – 1 tsp

Green chilli – 5 (slit and seeded)

Ghee – 1 tbsp (optional)

Salt – to taste

Method:

Boil lentils with turmeric. Peel and halve potatoes and add to the lentils. Peel onions and add to the pot together with green chillies and salt. When lentils and potatoes are cooked, fold in washed spinach leaves. Simmer for a few minutes, add ghee before serving.

———— ◆◆ ————

Torkari Diye Mooger Daal (split green gram with vegetables) | Serves four

Ingredients:

Split green gram (unroasted) – 250 gms

Green papaya – 200 gms

Potato – 200 gms

Ridge gourd – 200 gms

Drumstick – 2 or 3

Sunflower oil – 1 tbsp

Bay leaf – 2

Dried red chilli – 2 (whole)

Aniseed/ fennel seed – 1 tsp

Ginger paste – 1½ tsp

Salt & sugar – to taste

Method:

Cut the papaya and potatoes lengthwise. Boil the lentils and the vegetables separately. Blend the lentils well with a hand blender. Cut the ridge gourd and drumsticks into long pieces, add to the lentils and boil till done.

Add boiled papaya, potatoes and salt and sugar. When all vegetables are done, remove from heat.

In another pan, heat oil and fry the bay leaves, dried red chillies and fennel seeds, fry lightly, pour over the lentils.

- For a slightly bitter taste, add sliced bitter gourds along with the ridge gourd and drumsticks.
- A pinch of sugar adds to the taste.

Lau Diye Bhaja Mooger Daal (roasted split green gram with gourd)

Serves four

Ingredients:

Split green gram – 250 gms

Gourd – 500 gms

Turmeric powder/ paste – 1 tsp

Green chilli – 4 (slit and seeded)

Sunflower oil – 1 tbsp

Bay leaf – 2

Dried red chilli – 2 (whole)

Fenugreek seed – ½ tsp

Coriander leaf – a small bunch

Salt & sugar – to taste

Method:

Dry roast the lentils till they are golden. Cut bottle gourd into large pieces. Boil lentils, add turmeric and salt. When lentils and vegetables are done, add green chillies.

In another pan, heat oil and fry bay leaves, red chillies and fenugreek seeds, pour over the lentils. Add sugar to taste.

Garnish with chopped coriander leaves.

———— ◆◆ ————

Narkel Diye Chholar Daal (split bengal gram with coconut)

Serves four

Ingredients:

Split bengal gram – 250 gms

Raisin – 50 gms

Coconut (fresh) – ¼ cup (diced)

Turmeric powder/ paste – 1 tsp

Sunflower oil – 1 tbsp

Bay leaf – 2

Dried red chilli – 2 (whole)

Cumin seed – 1 tsp

Cinnamon – 2 (1" pieces)

Clove – 4

Green cardamom – 4

Salt & sugar – to taste

Method:

Soak raisins. Dice coconut finely, fry till light brown. Boil lentils and add raisins, fried coconut, turmeric, salt and sugar. Simmer for a few minutes.

Heat oil in another pan and toss in bay leaves, dried red chillies, cumin seeds, cinnamon, cloves and cardamoms. Pour the aromatic mix on to the lentils. Simmer till thick.

Mulo Diye Matar Daal (split pea lentils with white radish)

Serves four

Ingredients:

Split pea lentil – 250 gms

Horse radish – 2 (medium sized)

Tomato – 2 (chopped) optional

Broad bean – 100 gms

Green chilli – 4 (slit and seeded)

Sunflower oil – 1 tbsp

Bay leaf – 2

Dried red chilli – 2 (whole)

Onion seed – 1 tsp

Salt – to taste

Method:

Boil lentils, blend well with hand blender and add hot water. Add the cut radish, tomatoes, whole broad beans, green chillies and salt.

Cook till all vegetables are done. Heat oil in another pan and fry bay leaves, red chillies and onion seeds and pour over the lentils and mix well.

> Split green gram (moog daal) can be used instead, in which case cumin seeds should replace onion seeds.

Tauk Daal (sour lentils)

Serves four

Ingredients:

Split pea lentil – 200 gms

Raw mango – 2 (medium sized)

Green chilli – 3 or 4 (slit and seeded)

Sunflower oil – 1 tbsp

Bay leaf –2

Mustard seed – 1 tsp

Salt & Sugar – to taste

Method:

Boil lentils and add hot water to thin the broth. Peel and slice mangoes into thin strips and add to the lentils together with the chillies and salt. Cook till the mango is tender. Heat oil in another pan and toss in the bay leaves and mustard seeds. When the seeds crackle, pour over the boiled lentils. Lastly add sugar.

> Split green gram can be used instead of split pea lentils.

Matar Daaler Tarkari (vegetable curry with split pea lentils)

Ingredients:

Pith of plantain stem – 1 (small)

Red pumpkin – 200 gms

Mustard green –1 bunch

Brinjal – 150 gms (small sized)

Split pea lentil – 200 gms

Broad bean – 100 gms

Green chilli – 4 (slit and seeded)

Sunflower oil – 1½ tbsp

Bay leaf – 2 or 3

Dried red chilli – 2 (whole)

Mustard seed – 1 tsp

Ginger paste – 1 tsp

Aniseed/ fennel seed paste – 1 tsp

Salt & sugar – to taste

Method:

Slice the white pith of the plantain stem into thin circles. Care must be taken to remove the strings. Boil, drain and keep aside. Cut pumpkin into large pieces. Choose mustard greens with large leaves and retain the stems. Slit brinjals up to the stems.

Boil lentils and blend well with hand blender. Add to it, pumpkin, mustard greens, whole broad beans, green chillies and simmer till the vegetables are cooked. Add salt and lastly the brinjals. When brinjals are tender, add the cooked banana stems.

Heat oil in another pan and fry bay leaves, dried red chillies, mustard seeds and ginger and fennel seed pastes.

After a minute pour over the vegetable and lentils. Lastly add sugar.

Arhar Daal (split pigeon pea lentils)

Ingredients:

Split pigeon pea lentil – 250 gms

Turmeric powder/ paste – ¼ tsp

Bay leaf – 2 or 3

Sunflower oil – 1 tbsp

Dried red chilli – 3 or 4 (whole)

Mustard seed – ½ tsp

Dried mango powder (amchur) – 1½ tsp

Green chilli – 3 or 4 (slit and seeded)

Salt & sugar – to taste

Method:

Boil lentils with turmeric and bay leaves. Heat oil, fry the whole red chillies and mustard seeds and pour the lentils into this.

Add *amchur,* green chillies, salt and sugar and boil lentils for a few minutes.

Shona Mooger Daal (split green gram)

Ingredients:

Split green gram – 200 gms

Turmeric powder/ paste – ¼ tsp

Dried red chilli – 2 or 3 (whole)

Bay leaf – 2

Cumin seed – ½ tsp

Garam masala – 1 tsp (coarsely powdered)

Raisin – 50 gms, (soaked)

Coconut (fresh) – ½, (grated)

Green chilli – 3 or 4 (slit and seeded)

Ghee – 1 tbsp

Salt & sugar – to taste

Method:

Dry roast lentils and wash. Boil with turmeric. Heat oil in a pan and fry the dried red chillies, bay leaves, cumin seeds and garam masala. To this, add the mashed lentils. When the mixture comes to a boil, add raisins, coconut, green chillies, salt and sugar. Boil for a few minutes. Add ghee before serving.

Mushur Daal (red lentils)

Ingredients:

Red lentil – 250 gms

Turmeric powder/ paste – 1 tsp

Dried red chilli – 4 (whole)

Onion seed – 1 tsp

Green chilli – 3 or 4 (slit and seeded)

Sunflower oil – 1 tbsp

Salt & sugar – to taste

Method:

Boil and cook red split lentils with turmeric and a pinch of salt. Heat oil in a pan, add onion seeds and two dried red chillies, fry till chillies turn dark brown. Pour in the cooked lentils, bring to a boil, add salt, sugar and green chillies, boil for 2-3 minutes. Remove from fire.

OPTION II You can temper boiled red split lentils with fenugreek seed, dry red chillies and chopped onions instead of onion seeds.

OPTION III Thinly sliced garlic may be fried brown and added to the daal, topped with chopped tomatoes and fresh coriander leaves.

Kalaier Daal (split black lentils)

Serves four

Ingredients:

Split black lentil – 200 gms

Ginger powder/ paste – 1 tsp

Asafoetida powder – ¼ tsp

Aniseed/ fennel seed – 1 tsp

Green chilli – 3 or 4 (slit and seeded)

Sunflower oil – 1 tbsp

Salt – to taste

Method:

Boil and cook split black lentils with a pinch of salt. Heat oil in a pan, reduce heat, add asafoetida, aniseed and ginger pastes, fry. Pour in the cooked split black lentils, salt and green chillies, simmer for 3 minutes. Remove from fire.

◆◆

Enchor Diye Chholar Daal (split bengal gram with raw jackfruit)

Ingredients:

Raw jackfruit (*enchor*) – 250 gms

Split Bengal gram – 250 gms

Chilli powder/ paste – 1 tsp

Turmeric powder/ paste – 1 tsp

Oil – 1 tbsp

Coriander powder/paste – 1 tsp

Cumin powder/paste – 1 tsp

Bay leaf –2

Red chilli – 2

Cinnamon – 3 pieces (1″)

Cloves – 3

Green cardamoms – 3

Salt & sugar – to taste

Method:

Serves four

Before cutting jackfruit, smear oil on hands and fingers to avoid stickiness.

Remove hard outer skin, seeds and inner fibrous portions of the jackfruit, and the hard shells of seed pods.

Cut jackfruit into large cubes and boil.

Boil *daal*, add hot water, jackfruit, chilli, turmeric and salt.

Heat oil in another pan and first fry the coriander and cumin, then add bay leaves, red chillies, cinnamon, cloves and cardamoms.

Fry a minute or two, and then pour the *daal* over this.

Add sugar and mix well.

• Boiled potato cubes can be added along with the jackfruit pieces.

Bhaja

Bhajar Maja

– fries to die for

The Bengali bon vivant just has to have something fried with rice and lentils. Or else the meal is not quite complete. Almost all vegetables can be made into crispy fries. Peels, leaves, flowers and vegetable seeds, are all put to use. The fastidious foodie will appreciate a perfect match, of the fried items with the *daal* of the day. Think of fried balls of poppy seeds with black lentils *(kalaier daal)*, batter-fried eggplant with split green gram lentils *(moog daal)*, and fried potatos, mango fish or 'mourala' fish with red lentils *(mushur daal)*. *Khichuri* goes exceptionally well with as assortment of piping hot fries on a rainy day. The all time monsoon favourite is fried hilsa roe. Anything fried in the shape of balls are called *boraas*. The batter for the crisp fries can be made from besan (chickpea flour or gram flour), ground pulses, flour or rice powder. Fries are eaten best – piping hot!

* *"Rotis, luchis, fries of all kinds*

things sour, hot and sweet

are confectioners delights?"

──── RECIPES ────

Beguni (brinjal fritters)

Ingredients:

Brinjal – 300 gms (medium-sized)

Gram flour *(besan)* – 200 gms

Ginger paste – ½ tsp

Green chilli – 3 (chopped)

Poppy seed – 1 tsp

Mustard oil – 200 gms

Salt – to taste

Method:

Slice the brinjals lengthwise into thin slivers. Mix the gram flour, salt and water to make a batter. Beat well. Mix in the ginger paste and green chillies. Keep aside for half an hour. Add poppy seeds.

Dip the brinjals in the batter, one slice at a time and deep fry in hot oil till golden brown.

Begun Bhaja (fried brinjal)

Ingredients:

Brinjal – 400 gms (3 medium sized)

Salt & sugar – to taste

Turmeric powder/ paste – ½ tsp

Mustard oil – 150 gms

Method:

Slice the brinjals in rounds.

Smear the pieces with salt, sugar, and turmeric. Heat the oil, then fry the brinjals slices over a low flame till they are browned.

Mourala Machh Bhaja (white bait)

Ingredients:

Mola carplet/ White bait – 250 gms

Turmeric powder/ paste– 1 tsp

Mustard oil – 200 gms

Salt – to taste

Method:

De-scale the fish and wash thoroughly. Marinate with salt and turmeric. Heat oil and deep fry the fish till golden and crisp.

Dumo-Dumo Aalu Bhaja (fried potato cubes)

Serves four

Ingredients:

Potato – 400 gms (medium-sized)

Mustard oil – 2 tbsp

Green chilli – 2-3 (slit and seeded)

Onion seed – ½ tsp

Salt – to taste

Method:

Peel potatoes and cut them into small cubes. Heat oil and fry onion seeds and green chillies. Add potato cubes, fry and add salt.

Lower the flame and cover the pan. From time to time, uncover the pan, stir the potatoes, then cover again. Potatoes should be golden brown.

Lauer Khosha Bhaja (fried gourd peel)

Serves four

Ingredients:

Gourd peel – 1 cup

Mustard oil – 1½ tbsp

Dried red chilli – 2

Onion seed – ½ tsp

Poppy seed – 2 tsp

Salt – to taste

Method:

Wash gourd peels and cut into thin slivers. Boil slightly and drain.

Heat oil and fry red chillies and black onion seeds. Add the peels and stir fry.

When well fried, sprinkle poppy seeds and salt. Stir till evenly mixed.

> Potato peels can be fried in the same manner.

Kumror Phul Bhaja (pumpkin flowers fritters)

Serves four

Ingredients:

Red pumpkin flower – 16

Gram flour – 100 gms

Onion seed – 1 tsp

Mustard oil – 100 gms

Salt – to taste

Method:

Remove the stems from the pumpkin flowers and wash.

Make a batter with gram flour, salt and onion seeds. Dip the pumpkin flowers in the batter one by one and deep fry till golden.

Jhuro Aalu Bhaja (fried potato juliennes)

Serves four

Ingredients:

Potato – 400 gms (medium-sized)

Mustard oil – 200 gms

Salt – 1 tsp

Method:

Peel potatoes and cut them into thin strips. Alternately, grate potatoes. Soak the potato juliennes in water with salt.

After 10 minutes, squeeze and spread out to dry.

Deep fry the potato juliennes in hot oil over a high flame till golden.

Bok Phuler Bora (sesbania flower fritters)

Serves four

The white sesbania flower is also used in South East Asian cuisine

Ingredients:

Sesbania flower – 16

Gram flour – 100 gms

Onion seed – ½ tsp

Mustard oil – 100 gms

Salt – to taste

Method:

Wash sesbania flowers well, keeping the stems intact. Add salt and onion seeds to the gram flour, add water to make a batter.

Dip the sesbania flowers in the batter one by one and deep fry till golden brown.

Loita Machher Bora (bombay duck fritters)

Serves four

Ingredients:

Loita fish (Bombay duck) – 500 gms

Onion – 200 gms (chopped)

Garlic – 6 flakes (chopped)

Green chilli – 4 (chopped)

Flour – 2 tbsp

Gram flour – 2 tbsp

Mustard oil – 200 gms

Salt – to taste

Method:

Clean and wash the fish. Smear with salt and simmer in water.

Remove bones and mash. Mix in all ingredients except for the oil.

Form balls and deep fry in hot oil till well browned.

Kanthal Bichir Bora (jackfruit seed fritters)

Serves four

Ingredients:

Jackfruit seed – 1 cup

Green chilli – 1 tsp (Chopped)

Ginger paste – 1 tsp

Split pea lentil (*matar daal*) – 2 tbsp (paste)

Mustard oil – 150 gms

Salt & sugar – to taste

Method:

Boil jackfruit seeds, remove skins and mash. Mix chopped green chillies, ginger paste, salt and sugar with the mashed seeds and lentil paste. Form small balls and deep fry.

Sajney Phuler Bora (drumstick flower fritters)

Serves four

Ingredients:

Drumstick flower – 200 gms

Green chilli – 2 (chopped)

Gram flour – 100 gms

Mustard oil – 100 gms

Salt – to taste

Method:

Simmer drumstick flowers. Mix flowers, green chillies, salt, gram flour and a little water. Form balls and deep fry.

Machher Dimer Bora (fish-egg fritters)

Serves four

Ingredients:

Roe of carp (rohu or *katla*) – 250 gms

Onion – 200 gms (chopped)

Ginger – 25 gms (chopped)

Green chilli – 2 or 3 (chopped)

Coriander leaf – ½ cup (chopped)

Turmeric powder/ paste – ½ tsp

Flour – 1½ tbsp

Mustard oil – 150 gms

Salt – to taste

Method:

Mash the roe. Mix in all the ingredients except the oil.

Form balls from this mixture and deep fry in hot oil till they are golden and crisp.

Dhoney Patar Bora (coriander leaf fritters)

Serves four

Ingredients:

Coriander leaf – 3 bundles

Green chilli – 2 (chopped)

Poppy seed – 1 tsp

Gram flour (besan) – 4 tsp

Oil – 100 gms

Salt – to taste

Method:

Wash coriander leaves well and chop. Mix together chopped coriander leaves, green chillies, poppy seeds, salt and gram flour (besan).

Form into balls and deep fry.

Postor Bora (poppy seed fritters)

Serves four

Ingredients:

Poppy seed – 150 gms

Onion – 150 gms (chopped)

Green chilli – 3 (chopped)

Flour – 2 tsp

Mustard oil – 200 gms

Salt – to taste

Method:

Wash poppy seeds well and grind into a coarse paste.

Add salt, chopped onions, chillies and flour. Form balls and deep fry till golden.

Narkel Bora (coconut fritters)

Serves four

Ingredients:

Coconut (fresh) – 1 medium (grated)

Green chilli – 4 (finely chopped)

Rice flour – 2 tbsp

Aniseed/ fennel – 1 tsp

Mustard oil – 150 gms

Salt – to taste

Method:

Dry roast aniseed, grind to powder. Mix all the ingredients with grated coconut. Make balls and deep fry, Serve hot with chutney made from coriander leaves.

Daaler Bora (lentils fritters)

Ingredients:

Split pea lentils (matar daal) – 250 gms

Green chilli – 4 (finely chopped)

Onion – 2 large (finely chopped)

Asafotida – a pinch

Mustard oil – 150 gms

Salt – to taste

Method:

Wash *daal* and soak overnight. Grind *daal* to make a thick paste. Mix all ingredients except mustard oil. Make balls from lentil paste, deep fry and serve hot with mint or coriander chutney.

Topshe Fry (fried mango fish)

Ingredients:

Mango fish – 8 (standard sized)

Turmeric powder/ paste– 1 tsp

Red chilli paste – 1 tsp

Ginger paste – 3 tsp

Onion paste – 2 tbsp

Flour – 1 tbsp

Gram flour (besan) – 100 gms

Mustard oil – 200 gms

Salt – to taste

Method:

Dress and wash the fish. Smear with salt, turmeric, chilli powder and ginger and onion paste. Leave aside for an hour.

Mix together flour, gram flour and salt add water to make a batter.

Coat the fish with this batter and deep fry till golden.

Split pigeon peas powder (chhattu) can be used instead of besan to prepare fries or hand-made bread.

Charchchari

Charchchari, Ghonto & Chhokka
– tempting side dishes

It is nearly mid day, I am standing in the kitchen in New Delhi with my mother-in-law, Nivedita Sen. She painstakingly pares cauliflower stalks into thin slices. Deft with the kitchen knife, her tapering fair fingers chop the stems of spinach and radish leaves into perfect even sized pieces. "Never throw the waste bits away, store them in the fridge." I said cheekily "the end bits are rubbish". "You'll see how delicious these are when I make a *charchchari*". In a while she hands me bowl, "taste it" she says. I taste a spoonful and say "Give me more"!

This genre of food was born in the kitchens of rural Bengal. It was the discovery of the *'bous'* (the wives of the *babus*). The men went to work after a bellyful of rice, lentils, fish and other tasty morsels. After tiresome household chores, when the wives sat down to lunch, late afternoon, there was hardly anything substantial left for them to enjoy. Thus, the ladies conceptualized this dish. A fulfilling and finger-licking stir-fry to enjoy at leisure over chitchats and local gossip.

This preparation is a hotch potch of chopped vegetables, roots and succulent spinach stalks, shoots, fish heads (if available), jackfruit seeds, shoots, shrimps, crab claws, cockles, liver pieces and any other morsels that may have been aimed at the dustbin! When made by a skilled hand, a delicious *charchchari* is irresistible. It is also filling and nutritious.

Every Bengali household claims its own version. An aunt, or grandmother, a mother-in-law or a mother, may have bequeathed a special recipe to the family. The secret is handed down to the next generation. Often by word of mouth. Bengali widows in the olden days shunned meat or fish, so vegetarian *charchcharis* were a speciality created by them. It was not left to maids or cooks to mishandle this treat. The simple *charchchari* sprouted many variants, each suitable to a particular time, place, season and occasion. The variations are: *bati charchchari, chechki, sada charchchari, ghonto* and *chhanchra*. Ask any Bengali and each will claim that the taste of any of these delicacies, depends on the expert 'touch' of the maker! Knowing the art of cutting the vegetables for the *charchchari* is essential. In fact, it is sacrosanct to vary the chopping, paring, peeling (or not peeling) in order to create a deliciously satisfying and suitable *charchchari*.

"*Sadher lau banailo more bairagi*
Lauer aaga khailam doga go khailam…" *
— Bengali folk song

* "*The precious gourd was cooked by the wandering sage for me …*
I devoured the shoots, swallowed the stems, savoured the pot-pourri"

Tips

- Place a dry peeled garlic clove in the corner of the kitchen cupboard to keep ants away.

- Rub a piece of potato on the mixer grinder after grinding onions and garlic, this keeps away bad odour. Wash the gadget with soap and water afterwards.

- Before cutting vegetables into thin slices, soak the sharp knife in hot water for a few minutes. This makes chopping easier.

---------- RECIPES ----------

Bati Charchchari (stir fried vegetables) | Serves four

Ingredients:

Potato – 400 gms (diced)

Green chilli – 4/6

Turmeric powder/ paste – 2 tsp

Mustard oil – 1 tbsp

Salt – to taste

A bowl *(baati)* or pot which can be covered tightly.

> *'Baati'* means a bowl in Bengal

Method:

Mix all ingredients together in a bowl, keep aside one teaspoon of mustard oil to use later. Cover the bowl, simmer on a low fire till the potatoes are done, before taking the bowl off the fire, drizzle mustard oil on top.

Additions that make *bati charchchari* even more delectable: fresh green chopped mustard leaves *(shorshey shaak)*, long thin gourd finely chopped, chopped onions, fresh green peas. A handful of shrimps may be added for extra flavour. Freshly ground mustard seed paste, added to the mix can give the *bati charchchari* a nose tickling zest.

Bou Charchchari

(simple fried vegetables) | Serves four

Method:

The leftover stems and stalks of assorted spinach, cauliflowers, radishes, potato and pumpkin peels must be thoroughly cleaned. These remnants are cut finely and fried together in mustard oil with a bit of coriander, cumin, turmeric, red chilli paste, salt and sugar. This is a stir fried dish, quite nutritious and high in fibre and goes well with rice.

Khosha Charchchari

(stir fry made of peels) | Serves four

Method:

This variation comprises peels of assorted vegetables. Also very tasty and nutritious. The skins of potatoes, pumpkins, brinjals, gourd etc. are rich in vitamins. Peels should be finely cut and stir fried in oil with chillies, turmeric, whole poppy seeds, salt and a pinch of sugar. The pot-pourrie is enjoyed with plain rice.

> **Tips:** Rub your hands with potato peels to remove stains of turmeric.

Shaak Charchchari (spinach stir fry) | Serves four

Any spinach variety may be used such as *Kalmi shaak, Data shaak, Lal shaak, Kochu shaak, Sajney shaak, Notey shaak* and other seasonal spinaches. The spinach leaves must be washed carefully. Wilted or discoloured leaves should be discarded, the stalks or stems should be stripped off and the inner pulp, cut into 3" long sticks, the spinach roots may be used after cleaning and scraping off the soil and washed throughly.

Ingredients:

Potato – 150 gms (cut into long wedges, un peeled)
Red pumpkin – 150 gms (cut to suit the length of the potatoes)
Brinjal – 150 gms
Sweet potato – 100 gms
Parval – 100 gms
Horse radish (in winter) – 2 (medium)
Jackfruit seed – 10 (peeled and quartered)
Dried red chilli – 4 (whole)
Panchphoron – 1 tsp
Turmeric powder/paste – ½ tsp
Ginger paste – 1 tsp
Coriander powder/paste – 1 tsp
Cumin seed powder/paste – 1 tsp
Mustard oil – 2 tbsp
Salt & sugar – to taste.

Method:

In a large wok, heat mustard oil. When oil smokes, break red chillies, add *panch phoron*. When seeds splutter, add all the vegetables, stir well, next add all the spices. Lastly, add spinach leaves, shoots and stems.

Fry fast and quick, scraping the bottom of the pan, sprinkle water from time to time, to keep from sticking to the bottom. Add salt and sugar. Cover the pan, cook in low fire till done.

The *shaak charchchari* and *baati charchchari* are best eaten with hot plain rice.

A spinach *charchchari* is irresistible when shrimps, crab legs or lobster heads are added.

---- 🦢 ----

Paanch Mishali Charchchari (stir fried mixed vegetables) | Serves four
Method:

Same as above can be cooked without spinach. No need to add ginger and coriander or cumin paste. Just *panch phoron* and vegetables like potatoes, red pumpkins, brinjals and parvals will suffice. This is essentially a vegetarian dish. Serve hot with rice or *luchi, rotis* or *parathas*.

NB. *Lau* or gourd is hardly ever used in a *charchchari*.

Aalu Potoler Charchchari (stir fried potato-parval) | Serves four

Ingredients:

Potato – 250 gms

Parval – 250 gms

Panch phoran – 1 tsp

Dried red chilli – 2 (whole)

Turmeric powder/ paste – 1tsps

Red chilli powder/ paste – ½ tsp

Cumin powder/ paste – 1 tsp

Corinder powder/ paste – 1½ tsp

Mustard oil – 25 gms

Green chilli – 2 (slit)

Salt & sugar – to taste

Method:

Wash, peel and cut potatoes lengthwise like fingers. Scrape the skin of parvals (*potol*) and cut into long halves. Heat oil in pan, add *panch phoron*, dried red chillies and fry till brown. Add potato and parval, fry for five minutes in low heat, then add turmeric, cumin, coriander and chilli with sugar, fry for a minute, sprinkle some water from time to time, and fry for another five minutes. Now add green chilli and salt, pour a cup of water, cover and cook in low heat till done.

Bhindi Charchchari (stir fried okra) | Serves four

Ingredients:

Okra – 250 gms

Onion seed – 1 tsp

Dried red chilli – 2 (whole)

Turmeric powder/ paste – 1tsps

Red chilli powder/ paste – 1 tsp

Mustard paste – 2 tbsp

Mustard oil – 25 gms

Green chilli – 4 (slit & seeded)

Salt – to taste

Method:

Wash okra (*dhanrosh*) thoroughly, drain and dry, discard stem and cut into one inch long pieces. Mix turmeric and red chilli in a bowl with water keep aside.

Heat oil in pan, add onion seeds, dried red chillies and fry till brown. Add okra fry for 2 minutes. Pour turmeric and red chilli mixture, salt, cover and cook till tender. Add mustard paste and green chillies. Cook till done. Raw mangoes in season add a piquant flavour to the dish.

Tips: Rub the knife with newspaper if it gets slippery after cutting okras, this helps to keep the knife clean and can be washed easily with soap water.

Bhetki Machher Kanta Charchchari
(stir fried vegetables with beckti bones)

Ingredients:

Bone of Beckti – 500 gms

(Central bone of Beckti with flakes or bits of the fish, cut into 2" bits)

Potato – 200 gms (sliced)

Onion – 200 gms (sliced)

Ginger paste – 2 tsp

Garlic paste – 1 tsp

Onion seed – 1 tsp

Mustard oil – 3 tbsp

Green chilli – 4 (slit and seeded)

Mustard paste – 50 gms (optional)

Salt & sugar – to taste.

Method:

Fry beckti pieces, Keep aside. Heat oil, add onion seeds. When seeds splutter, add all ingredients with potatoes and fry well. Now add fried fish pieces, cover and simmer till done. Serve with rice.

Liver Charchchari (liver stir fry)

Ingredients:

Liver – 200 gms (cut into small bits)

Potato – 250 gms (diced)

Onion paste – 2 tbsp

Ginger paste – 1 tbsp

Garlic paste – 1 tsp

Tomato – 150 gms (cut in to small pieces)

Onion – 100 gms (chopped)

Mustard oil – 1 ½ tbsp

Green chilli – 4 (chopped)

Salt – to taste.

Method:

Heat oil, add chopped onions and tomatoes, stir till soft, then add the pastes, fry till brown. Add liver and potatoes and fry well. Lastly, add the chillies and salt, stir again, add a cup of water. Cover till potatoes are done. Liver hardens when over cooked, so lower the heat after the potatoes are soft. Garnish with coriander leaves and serve.

Rasun Charchchari (garlic stir fry)

Serves four

(This stir fried item tastes good when made with winter vegetables. Not authentically Bengali, this recipe may have its origins in Darjeeling and Nepalese kitchens.)

Ingredients:

Fiddlehead (*dheki shaak*) a seasonal

spinach – a bunch

Beetroot – 200 gms (finely chopped)

Cabbage leaf – 100 gms (finely chopped)

Potato – 200 gms (diced)

Red pumpkin – 150 gms (diced)

Brinjal – 150 gms

Tomato – 200 gms (finely chopped)

Garlic paste – 1 tbsp

Red chilli powder/ paste – 2 tsp

Panch phoron – 1 tsp

Turmeric powder/ paste – ½ tsp

Mustard oil – 1 tsp

Salt – to taste

Method:

Heat oil in a pan. Add a pinch of *panch phoron*, when it splutters, add all other ingredients and stir well, sprinkle water, cover and cook till done. Serve with rice. This preparation is enhanced with lots of fresh 'red chillies'.

———— CHECHKI ————

This variation is similar to a *charchchari*, except that a *chechki* fry is restricted to one or most two kinds of vegetables. Finely slice the selected vegetables, heat mustard oil in a pan, add a teaspoon of mustard seeds and one or two dry red chillies, add sliced vegetables and fry with a pinch of sugar to bring out the flavours of the vegetables.

A *chechki* may be made of potatoes or pumpkins. It may be made with *'thor'* (banana stalks), or radishes. Sometimes fresh winter radish leaves, can be used with ginger.

Mulo Chechki (stir fried radish)

Serves four

Ingredients:

Horse radish – 500 gms

Mustard seed – 1 tsp

Dried red chilli – 3 (whole)

Mustard oil –1 tbsp

Salt & sugar – to taste

Method:

Wash, peel and chop radish finely. Heat oil in a pan tempered with mustard seed and red chillies. Add chopped radish with a pinch of sugar, stir fry for five minutes, then add salt. Stir briskly and cook till done. Remove from fire.

Kumro Chechki (stir fried red pumpkin)

Ingredients:

Red pumpkin – 500 gms

Mustard seed – 1 tsp

Dried red chilli – 3 (whole)

Mustard oil –1 tbsp

Salt & sugar – to taste

Method:

Chop pumpkin into fine, thin slices. Heat oil in a pan tempered with mustard seed and red chillies, add pumpkin with a pinch of sugar, stir fry for a few minutes, then add salt, stir frequently and cook for another 7-8 minutes till done. Remove from fire.

──── GHONTO ────

Ghonto is similar to the *charchchari* usually made with a few extra ingredients to give it a special flavour. These ingredients are ginger paste, *radhuni* and *bori* (dried lentil balls).

Lau Ghonto (gourd curry)

Ingredients:

Gourd – 1 kg

Cumin seed – 1 tsp

Dried lentil ball (Bori) – 25 gms

Bay leaf – 2 pcs

Green chilli – 4 (slit & seeded)

Flour – 2 tsp (optional)

Cooking oil – 2 tbsp

Garam masala powder/ paste – 1tsp

Ghee – 1 tbsp

Salt & sugar – to taste

Method:

Wash, peel and grate gourd. Boil gourd and squeeze out water. Fry *boris* and keep aside. Heat oil, add cumin seeds, bay leaves and fry. Now put steamed gourd with fried *boris*, sugar and salt, stir fry in low heat. Add green chillies, stir fry. Add flour with a little water and cook till dry. Add *garam masala* with ghee before removing from fire.

Mocha Ghonto (banana flower with coconut and potato) | Serves four

Ingredients:

Banana flower – 1 (whole)

Potato – 2 medium (200 gm)

Coconut (fresh) – ½ (finely chopped)

Cumin seed – 1 tsp

Bay leaf – 2 pcs

Green chilli – 4 (slit & seeded)

Ginger paste – 1 tsp

Mustard oil – 20 gms

Garam masala powder/ paste – 1tsp

Ghee – 1tbsp

Salt & sugar – to taste

Method:

Wash, peel and cut potatoes into small cubes. Remove deep purple outer skin from each banana flower. Pluck centre of flower and remove the pollen tube and chop the flowers very finely. Fry potatoes lightly and keep aside.

Fry chopped coconut till brown and keep aside. Boil chopped banana flower with a little salt, squeeze and drain. Heat oil in a pan till it smokes, add cumin seed, bay leaves and fry.

Now add steamed banana flower, ginger paste, sugar and salt, stir fry on low heat. Add green chillies, fried potatoes and coconut, cover the pan and cook on a low flame. Add *garam masala* and ghee before removing from fire.

Mulo Ghonto (radish curry) | Serves four

Ingredients:

Horse radish – 500 gms (medium size)

Cumin seed – 1 tsp

Bay leaf – 2 pcs

Green chilli – 4 (slit & seeded)

Flour – 2 tsp (optional)

Mustard oil – 20 gms

Garam masala powder/ paste – 1tsp

Ghee – 1 tbsp

Salt & sugar – to taste

Method:

Wash, peel and grate radish. Boil radish and squeeze water out. Heat oil in a pan add cumin seeds, bay leaves and fry. Now put boiled radish with sugar and salt, stir fry on low heat. Add green chillies and fry for few minutes more. Add flour with a little water and stir till dry. Add *garam masala* with ghee before removing from fire.

Machher Maathar Muri Ghonto (fish head with rice and vegetables)

Ingredients:

Fish head (rohu/katla) – 1 large

Potato – 250 gm (medium sized)

Parval (*Potol*) – 200 gms

Basmati rice – 50 gms

Turmeric powder/ paste – 1 ½ tsp

Red chilli powder/ paste – 1 tsp

Onion paste – 1 tbsp

Ginger paste – 1 ½ tsp

Bay leaf – 2 pcs

Green chilli – 2 (slit & seeded)

Mustard oil – 100 gms

Garam masala whole – 4 green cardamom, 4 cloves and 1"cinnamon

Garam masala powder/ paste – 1tsp

Ghee – 1 tbsp

Salt & sugar – to taste

Method:

Serves four

Wash rice, drain and spread to dry. Wash, peel and cut potatoes and parval (*potol*) into halves. Lightly fry potatoes and parvals (*potol*) and keep aside.

Wash, clean and remove gills from fish head. Smear fish head with a little turmeric and salt, fry lightly and keep aside. Heat oil and put whole *garam masalas* and bay leaves, fry. Add onions and ginger, fry for a minute, then add turmeric and chilli powder/ paste with a little water and sugar, stir fry till the spices release oil.

Add rice and stir fry for 2 minutes, add fried potatoes and parval (*potol*), fry for another minute, add fried fish heads, breaking them into pieces, and fry for another 2 minutes. Add water and salt. Cook on a slow fire for 5 minutes till done. Finally, add *garam masala* with ghee and serve.

———— CHANCHRA ————

This *charchchari* variation is a totally non-vegetarian dish. A truly authentic Bengali *chanchra* must be made with fish heads of carp or *Rui*, hilsa or *Ilish*. Freshly picked succulent *pui, lau* or *notey saag,* mixed with turmeric, coriander and cumin powder, tempered with five mix seeds (*panch phoron*) and the fish heads – make this famous Bengali dish fit for any celebratory occasion.

—————— CHHOKKA ——————

This variation is to be had with *luchis* (fried flour bread or puris) or *rootis* (flatbread) and is generally eaten at dinner. A good *chhokka* is usually made with diced ripe, sweet red pumpkins, potatoes, and parvals *(potols)*, sometimes soaked chick-peas/ Bengal gram are added to make it a substantial dish.

Kumror Chhokka (red pumpkin with chick peas) | Serves four

Ingredients:

Red pumpkin – 300 gms
Potato – 250 gms
Parval – 250 gms
Chick-pea/ Bengal gram – ½ cup
Ginger paste – 1tbsp
Turmeric powder/ paste – 1 tsp
Coriander powder/ paste – 1tsp
Red chilli powder/ paste – 1 tsp
Dried red chilli – 2 (whole)
Panch phoron – 1 tsp
Bay leaf – 2 pcs
Garam masala paste – 1 tsp
Mustard oil – 50 gms
Salt & sugar – to taste

Method:

Soak chick-peas or Bengal gram over night. Wash, peel and dice red pumpkin, potatoes and parval *(potol)*. Fry potato, pumpkin and parval *(potol)* lightly and separately, keep aside. Add oil and fry bay leaves, *panch phoron* and whole red chillies. Mix turmeric, coriander, chilli and ginger with sugar and a little water. Fry till spices release oil, now add fried potato, pumpkin, parval and soaked peas with salt, sprinkle some water and simmer on a low heat till done. Add *garam masala* and serve.

Tips

- Add a teaspoon of salt to water while boiling potatoes with peels It locks in the flavour and keeps potatoes firm.

- To keep away ants from the sugar bowl, place 2-3 pieces of cloves inside container.

Daalna & Dolma

Daalna & Dolma Delights
– vegetable variations

*"Appetites of stomach and the palate, far from diminishing
as man grows older go on increasing"*

— Cicero (106-43 BC)

Daalna is a pleasant variation of a vegetable curry. A perfect recipe for summer vegetables, though any vegetable or substitute will do. The basic gravy is wonderfully versatile and it special because *daalna* is cooked without garlic and liberally spiced with aromatic spices. Fresh ginger, cumin, coriander, *garam masala*, bay leaves, cinnamon, cloves and cardamom enhance this variety of vegetable curry and imbue, even the most bland and boring vegetables, with an irresistible flavour. It is not known where or how the *daalna* originated, but it is considered a 'special' delight to please fastidious vegetarians.

RECIPES

Phulkopir Daalna (cauliflower curry)

| Serves four

Ingredients:

Cauliflower – 500 gms
Potato – 250 gms
Cumin seed – 1 tsp
Bay leaf – 2 pcs
Cumin powder/ paste – 1½ tsp
Coriander powder/ paste – 1½ tsp
Red chilli powder/ paste – 1 tsp
Ginger paste – 1tbsp
Turmeric powder/ paste – 1 tsp
Green cardamom & Clove – 4 (each)
Cinnamon – 2 inch
Mustard oil – 2 tbsp
Garam masala powder/ paste – 1 tsp
Ghee – 1 tbsp
Salt & sugar – to taste

Method:

Wash, peel and cut potatoes into quarters. Wash cauliflower and cut into florets. Fry cauliflowers and potatoes lightly and keep aside. Heat oil in a pan, add cumin seed, bay leaves, cardamoms, cloves and cinnamon, fry lightly. Add cumin, coriander, chilli, turmeric and ginger with a little water and fry well. Add fried cauliflower and potatoes with salt and sugar, fry for 2 minutes on low heat. Pour two cups of water and cook till done. Top with *garam masala* and ghee. Serve hot with rice.

- In winter, fresh green peas can be added.

Oaler or Peper Daalna (arum/ green papaya curry)

| Serves four

Ingredients:

Arum/ green papaya – 500 gms
Potato – 250 gms
Cumin seed – 1 tsp
Bay leaf – 2 pcs
Cumin powder/ paste – 1½ tsp
Coriander powder/ paste – 1½ tsp
Ginger paste – 1 tbsp
Turmeric powder/ paste – 1 tsp
Red chilli powder/ paste – 1 tsp

Method:

Wash, peel and cut vegetables into medium sized cubes. Boil vegetables till half done and drain. Lightly fry boiled vegetables and keep aside. Heat oil in a pan, add cumin seeds, bay leaves, cardamoms, cloves and cinnamon, fry lightly. Add cumin, coriander, chilli, turmeric and ginger pastes with a little water. Fry lightly and then add fried vegetables with salt and sugar, fry for

Green cardamom – 4	
Clove – 4	
Cinnamon – 2 inch	
Mustard oil – 2 tbsp	
Garam masala powder/ paste – 1 tsp	
Ghee – 1 tbsp	
Salt & sugar – to taste	

2 minutes in low heat. Add a cup of water and cook till done. Garnish with *garam masala* and ghee and serve.

OPTION:
Add a dash of tamarind juice to make a tangy curry.

Enchorer Daalna (green jackfruit curry)

Serves four

Ingredients:

Green jackfruit – 500 gms
Potato – 250 gms
Cumin seed – 1 tsp
Bay leaf – 2 pcs
Cumin powder/ paste – 1½ tsp
Coriander powder/ paste – 1½ tsp
Red chilli powder/ paste – 1 tsp
Ginger paste – 1tbsp
Turmeric powder/ paste – 1 tsp
Green cardamom – 4
Clove – 4
Cinnamon – 2"
Mustard oil – 2 tbsp
Garam masala powder/ paste – 1tsp
Ghee – 1tbsp
Salt & sugar – to taste

Method:

Wash, peel and cut potatoes into cubes. Peel, clean and cut green jackfruit in the same manner, boil till half done and drain. Lightly fry potatoes and boiled jackfruit and keep aside. Heat oil in a pan add cardamoms, cloves, cumin seeds, bay leaves, and cinnamon, fry lightly. Add cumin, coriander, chilli, turmeric and ginger pastes with little water and fry till spices are done. Add potatoes and green jackfruit with salt and sugar, fry for 2 minutes in low heat. Add two cups of water and cook till done. Top with *garam masala* and ghee before serving.

OPTION:

Green jackfruit can be cooked with garlic, ginger and onion pastes together with the other ingredients mentioned above, to make a rich and tasty curry. The green jackfruit is considered 'meat from the trees', it tastes delicious when treated like meat.

Yoghurt can be used in the recipe above. Ghee is optional in all these recipes.

Dhokar Daalna (split pea lentil cake curry) | Serves four

Ingredients:

Matar daal – 500 gms
Potato – 250 gms
Mustard oil – 2 tbsp
Yoghurt – 200 gms
Green chilli – 4 (slit and seeded)
Garlic paste – 1 tbsp
Cumin seed powder/ paste – 1tsp
Red chilli powder/ paste – 1tsp
Ginger paste – 1tbsp
Ghee – 1 tsp
Bay leaf – 2
Asafoetida – 2 pinches
Soda bicarbonate – 1 pinch
Salt & sugar – to taste

Method:

Wash *daal* and soak overnight. Grind the *daal* to a paste. Mix a pinch of soda bicarbonate, salt, sugar, garlic paste. Heat oil in a pan add asafoetida, fry the paste till dry. Take a shallow plate or a platter with a 2" rim. Empty the mixture on to it. Press down with fingers so that the fried *daal* mix sets in, should be about 1" high. Next, cut the set mixture into squares.

Fry these squares gently in a pan, set aside. Next, fry the potatoes and keep aside. In the same pan add a little more oil, heat it, add a pinch of asafoetida, cumin seeds, bay leaves, ginger paste fry. Add yoghurt well beaten in a cup of water with red chilli and potatoes. When the potatoes are done, gently place the squares in the curry. Add ghee and green chillies before serving.

Chhanar Daalna (bengali cottage cheese curry) | Serves four

Ingredients:

For Chhana

Milk – 2 ltrs
Juice of one lemon or sour yoghurt – 1 tbsp
Cotton/ muslin bag or a square cloth

For the curry

Potato – 4 or 5 cut into pcs
Sunflower oil – 2 tbsp
Ghee (optional) – 1 tsp
Turmeric powder/ paste – 1 tsp

Method:

To make chhana: Boil milk in a sauce pan and add lemon juice or sour yoghurt into it. When milk curdles, pour into a muslin bag or make a cloth bundle and hang it up. Wait till all water has drained and the consistency is thick. Squeeze out all excess water.

Method for curry: Make small balls with the freshly made *chhana*. Squeeze again to drain excess water. If not firm add a bit of flour.

Cumin powder/ paste – 1 tsp

Coriander powder/ paste – 1 tsp

Ginger paste – 2 tsps

Bay leaf – 2

White cumin seed – ¼ tsp

Garam masala powder/ paste – ¼ tsp

Ghee – 1 tsp

Salt & sugar – to taste

Fry balls in oil and set aside. Fry the potatoes and set aside. In the same pan add bay leaves all the spices, except *garam masala*, fry for a minute, add water, season with salt and sugar. The potatoes go in first into the gravy, when they are tender, add the dumplings very gently, let them soak in the simmering gravy for a few minutes in low heat. Before serving add *garam masala* and ghee.

Aalu Potol Kumror Daalna (potato-parval-pumpkin curry) | Serves four

Ingredients:

Potato – 200 gms

Parval – 200 gms

Red pumpkin – 200 gms

Coriander seed – 2 tsp (roasted)

Cumin seed – 2 tsp (roasted)

Mustard oil – 3 tbsp

Bay leaf – 2

Green chilli – 4 (slit and seeded)

Cumin seed – 1 tsp

Poppy seed paste – ¾ cup

Ghee – 1 tsp

Garam masala powder – ½ tsp

Salt & sugar – to taste

Method:

Dice vegetables. Grind roasted spices. Heat oil in a pan, fry bay leaves, green chillies and cumin seeds. Put potatoes first and then the other vegetables and fry. Add spices and poppy seed paste, fry for a minute. Add salt, sugar and water, cover and cook till done. Add ghee and *garam masala* before removing from fire.

OPTION:

Potato and parvals can be used with whole pepper corn and raisins.

Dolma

– stuffed vegetables

> "*Dolma is a family of stuffed vegetable dishes found in the cuisines of the former Ottoman Empire and Europe, Russia, Iran, Central and South Asia. Perhaps the best-known is the grape-leaf dolma. Common vegetables to stuff include zucchini, eggplant, tomato and pepper. The stuffing may or may not include meat.*"
>
> — Wikipedia

This speciality may have had its origins in Europe, Greece and Middle East. Stuffed vine leaves are called dolmas. It may have arrived with the Moghul invasions to Eastern India. Any stuffed vegetable preparation is now labeled *dolma* in Bengal.

This particular item is considered a delicacy. The *'dolma'* is usually made with *'potol'* (parval). The *'potol'* is stuffed with tasty fillings, such as cooked flaky fish or minced shrimps, meat or cottage cheese, then fried and dropped into a *daalna* – like curry. *Dolma* requires special effort, thus it is not an everyday feature. It is a special occasion or festive dish, suited for a feast.

Machh Potoler Dolma (parval with fish stuffing)

Serves four

Ingredients:

For Stuffing

Potol (parval) – 8 large (400 gms)

Fish – 300 gms (*rui/ katla* or *bhetki* cut in to large pieces)

Raisins – 25 gms

Turmeric powder/ paste – 1 tsp

Red chilli powder/ paste – 1 tsp

Onion paste – 1 ½ tsp

Ginger paste – 1tbsp

Garam masala powder/ paste – 1 tsp

Toothpick – 8 pieces

Mustard Oil – 300 gms

Salt & sugar – to taste

For Curry

Ginger and onion paste – 2 tbsp

Mustard oil – 1 tbsp

Tomato – 2 (chopped)

Turmeric powder/ paste – 1 tsp

Salt & sugar – to taste

Method:

Soak raisins in a cup of water for 15 minutes. Scrape the skin of the parvals (*potol*), then cut one end and scoop out seeds to make a hollow. Make slits in the parvals with a sharp knife. Preserve the top end to use it as a lid or sealer.

To make the stuffing

Boil fish pieces with salt and turmeric. Drain, de-bone and mash the fish. Heat 2 tbsp oil in a pan, add onion and ginger paste, fry till light brown, then add mashed fish, chilli paste with 1 tsp sugar and salt, sprinkle a little water, add soaked raisins, fry for 2 minutes, then add *garam masala* and stir fry till the mixture becomes semi-dry. Fill the *potols/* parvals with fish and secure the top end with the cut piece, seal it with toothpicks. Fry stuffed *potols/* parvals in a shallow pan carefully.

The stuffing made with minced meat or shrimps is cooked in the same way.

The dry *dolma* is served best as an accompaniment to *daal*.

To make the curry

Fry ingredients till done, add water. When it comes to boil, put in the cooked *dolma*s, let it simmer for a few minutes, take it off the fire and serve with rice or *luchis*.

Khichuri

Khaasha Khichuri
– kedgeree delight

"The moog (daal) is boiled
with rice, and then buttered and eaten.
This is what they call – 'kishri'"

— Ibn Batuta, 1340 AD

Monsoon is such a romantic season. In summer, one waits longingly for it to arrive. Man and nature yearn for the solace of clouds and cascading showers. It's arrival is heralded with flashes of lightning, dark skies, stormy winds and the roar of thunder. The patter of raindrops are like tinkling anklets on a courtesans shimmering skirt. Tagore, the poet laureate of Bengal, has composed a multitude of lyrics and songs devoted to this romantic season.

The monsoon months are June, July, August and may last up to early September. The first rains are heavenly but alas we are earthly creatures. Man cannot live by romance alone! As always thoughts turn to 'what shall we eat today?' The downside of heavy rain is that one dreads venturing out into the muddy bazaars. The secret is to plan ahead for the rainy day. A few essentials are usually stored, in case water logged streets prevent one from stepping out. The basic rice, *daal*, oil and spices are stocked well ahead, as well as potatoes and fresh vegetables that can last in the fridge. These are all one needs to cook up the most popular item of the season – the ubiquitous *khichuri*.

Khichuri is a delicious one-pot preparation of rice, *daal* and whatever else you may wish to throw in to the mix! Served piping hot, accompanied with all sorts of crisp fries – it is the ultimate comfort food for a cool, windy and wet day. And here I may add, that, after a hearty meal of *khichuri*, the only activity one should indulge in, is a siesta!

— RECIPES —

Khichuri (kedgeree/ kichri)

Ingredients:

Rice – 150 gms

Split green gram (*moog*) – 150 gms

Potato – 4 (medium sized)

Green pea – ½ cup (shelled)

Coconut (fresh) – ½ (finely chopped)

Cooking oil – 2 tbsp

Ghee – 1 tbsp

Bay leaf – 4

Cumin seed – 1 tsp

Dried red chilli – 2 (whole)

Green chilli – 6 (slit and seeded)

Ginger – 1½" (finely chopped)

Garam masala (whole) – 4 cloves,
4 cardamom, cinnamon 1"

Salt & sugar – to taste

Method:

Wash, peel and cut potatoes into halves. Roast split green gram in a dry heated pan till light brown, and keep aside. (heat oil in a pan and fry chopped coconut to brown – optional), remove from oil and keep aside. Now pour more oil in the pan, heat till it smokes, add cumin seed, bay leaves, whole *garam masala* and red chillies, fry for 2 minutes. Add roasted split green gram and rice and ginger paste, fry for another 3 minutes. Pour enough water to cover the mixture, bring to boil. Add potatoes, salt and sugar and cook till half done. Now add green peas, green chillies and cook till done. Top with fried coconut and ghee, mix it well. Serve hot.

OPTION:

Khichuri may be made with *mushur daal* (red lentils). In summer parval or *potol* may be used, potatoes, whole onions. In winter, beans, tomatoes, cauliflowers etc are good.

Bhuni Khichuri (dry kedgeree)

The method and ingredients are the same as *khichuri* above (coconut is not needed), Cook it until the water has been absorbed and the *khichuri* is soft and moist.

Narkel Khichuri (split green gram kedgeree with coconut)

Serves four

Ingredients:

Coconut (fresh) – 1 (grated)

Basmati rice – 150 gms

Split green grams (*moog*) – 150 gms

Ghee or white oil – 2 tbsp

Bay leaf – 4

Cumin seed –1 tsp

Red chilli – 8

Potato – 4 (cut in large pieces)

Cauliflower – 10 large florets

Turmeric powder/ paste – 1 tsp

Ginger paste – 1½" tsp

Tomato – 2 (chopped)

Green pea – 1½ cups

Garam masala powder/ paste – 1 tsp

Salt & sugar – to taste

Method:

Extract two draws of coconut milk first.

Heat some of the ghee in a pan and fry the rice and split green gram. Pour in the second draw of coconut milk and boil till the rice and gram are half done.

In another pan, heat more ghee and fry the bay leaves, cumin seeds and red chillies for a few seconds. Add potato and cauliflower pieces and fry well.

To this add the half-cooked *khichuri*, salt and turmeric. Mix thoroughly.

Now add ginger, tomato, peas, sugar and the first draw of coconut milk. Simmer, stirring continuously to avoid the food at the bottom getting charred, till the ingredients are cooked and the *khichuri* is thick. Lastly, mix in the remaining ghee and *garam masala*.

Good accompaniments – hot curries, fries, papadoms and gossip!

Tips:
To make potato chips (*aalu bhaja*) crispy, while frying add little baking powder to oil.

Prawn Khichuri (roasted split green grams kedgeree with prawn) | Serves four

Ingredients:

Basmati rice – 200 gms

Split green gram (*moog*) – 200 gms (roasted)

Prawn – 250 gms (large)

Turmeric powder/ paste –1 tsp

Mustard oil – 3 tbsp

Bay leaf – 4

Cumin seed – 1 tsp

Onion – 200 gms (chopped)

Tomato – 150 gms, chopped

Ginger paste – 2 tbsp

Garlic paste – 2 tbsp

Cumin powder/ paste – 2 tbsp

Red chilli powder/ paste – 1½ tbsp

Green chilli – 10 (slit)

Ghee – 1 tbsp

Salt & sugar – to taste

Method:

Smear the prawns with salt and turmeric. Heat oil in a large pan and fry prawns till they turn pink. Keep prawns aside. In remaining oil add bay leaves, cumin seeds and the onions and fry. Next, add tomatoes and cook till soft. Add ginger, garlic, cumin and red chillies and fry till oil separates from spices. Now add rice and roasted split green gram and fry for a minute.

Pour hot water and stir well. When the water comes to a boil, add salt.

Cover and cook, stirring from time to time. When nearly done, add the fried prawns, green chillies and sugar. Add ghee before serving.

Tips:

- Potato is the world's most favourite vegetable . Five thousand varieties of potatoes are available throughout the world. Potato first came to England from South America and arrived in India during the British Raj. Potatoes contain Vitamins C and B6.

- Onions contain Vitamin C and minerals.   • Fresh ginger helps reduce nausea.

- Capsicum came from America, it contains Vitamin C, calcium, phosphorus and anti-oxidants.

Dimer Khichuri (red lentils kedgeree with egg)

Ingredients:

Basmati rice – 200 gms

Red lentil (*mushur*) – 200 gms

Onion – 250 gms

Green chilli – 6 (whole)

Egg – 4

Salt – to taste

Baking powder – ¼ tsp

Milk – 2 tbsp

Flour – 2 tsp

Mustard oil – 50 gms

Bay leaf – 4

Pepper corn – 10

Ginger paste – 4 tbsp

Cumin powder/ paste– 2 tbsp

Turmeric powder/ paste – 1½ tsp

Green pea – 1½ cups

Tomato – 250 gms

Ground black pepper – 2 tsp

Ghee – 2 tbsp

Salt & sugar – to taste

Method:

Beat the eggs. Finely chop one onion and 2 green chillies, add them to beaten eggs with salt, baking powder, milk and flour. Fry an omlette, cut in to pieces and keep aside.

Chop tomatoes and remaining onions; slit the remaining green chillis.

Heat oil, fry bay leaves and peppercorns. Add onions and fry till golden.

Add to this the ginger, cumin, turmeric, salt and sugar and fry till the oil separates from the spices. Now add the rice and lentils and keep frying.

Add hot water, when it comes to a boil, put peas, tomatoes and green chillies. Finally, add ground black pepper. At the time of serving, top with ghee and the omlette pieces.

Tips: Refrigerate food which has excess oil. Take out the oil from the top with a spoon. Now heat the food before eating, amount of oil in the food will be less.

Keema Khichuri (split green gram kedgeree with minced meat)

Ingredients:

Basmati rice – 200 gms

Split green gram (*moog*) – 200 gms (roasted)

Minced meat – 250 gms

Curd – 100 gms

White oil – 100 gms

Cumin seed – 1 tsp

Green cardamom – 4

Clove – 4

Cinnamon – 1"

Onion paste – 5 tbsp

Garlic paste – 1 tsp

Ginger paste – 4 tbsp

Cumin powder/ paste – 2 tbsp

Red chilli powder/ paste – 1 tbsp

Coriander Powder/ paste – 2 tsp

Turmeric powder/ paste – 1½ tsp

Tomato puree – 4 tbsp

Salt & sugar – to taste

Bay leaf – 4

Green chilli – 6 (slit and seeded)

Tomato – 100 gms (chopped)

Ghee – 4 tbsp

Garam masala powder – 2 tsp

Method:

Marinate the minced meat in curd with a pinch of turmeric for an hour.

Fry ginger, garlic, onion, coriander, cumin pastes, turmeric, tomato puree and sugar. Fry till oil floats up. Mix in minced meat and fry well till meat is almost done. In another pan, fry 1 tbsp of oil in a pan and fry half-teaspoon cumin seeds, whole cardamoms, cloves, bay leaves and cinnamon, rice and green gram (*moog daal*) also green chillies and chopped tomatoes. Add hot water together. When rice and daal are half cooked, blend in the minced meat. Garnish with ghee and *garam masala*.

———◆◆———

"*Indi, Bindi, Shindi climbed up a tree*
On a Saturday. From upon the tree they heard
Someone croon. A dreadful nasal me-lo-dy
The tune made Indi very hungry. He climbed down ever so quickly
To eat his mom's khichuri…"

– Popular old song

Dalia Khichuri (dalia kedgeree)

|Serves four

Ingredients:

Dalia (broken wheat) - ½ cup

Split green gram (moog) – ½ cup

Green peas – ½ cup (optional)

Onion – 2 (chopped)

Ginger – 1 tbsp (chopped)

Turmeric – 1 tsp

Bay leaf – 2

Dried red chili – 2 (whole)

Cumin seeds – 1 tsp

Cinnamon – 1"

Clove – 4 (whole)

Cardamom – 4 (whole)

Green chilli – 2 tsp (chopped)

White oil – 2 tbsp

Ghee – 1 tbsp (for garnishing)

Water – 3 cups

Salt & sugar – to taste

Method:

Wash and soak split green gram (*moog daal*) and *dalia* for 10 minutes and keep aside, till the cereals are tender. Heat oil in a pan and temper with bay leaves, cumin seeds, dried red chillies, cinnamon, cardamom and clove. Add onion, fry till brown. Then add ginger and turmeric fry for some time. Add *dalia,*split green gram and green peas (optional), fry for 2 minutes. Then pour water, green chillies, salt and sugar. Cover the pan, cook in low heat till done. Remove from fire, garnish with ghee and serve hot.

Tips:

• Smear mustard (or any other) oil on your hands before chopping banana flowers or jackfruit.

• Green chillies will remain fresh if the dry stems are discarded.

• Rub cooking oil on your hands before washing raw fish to keep away the smell of fish.

Jhol

Jampesh Jhol

– spicy stews

"Peter gondogol? Khao tobey jhol!" *

During the sultry summer months a bowl of light curried vegetables, more in the nature of a stew is de-rigueur. There are certain unwritten norms regarding the Bengali diet. The long, hot summer is the season for mild curried stews. It cools the head, soothes the stomach and sustains the body. Summer apart, stress and strain of journeys, household problems and domestic crises call for *jhols*. Bengali epicurean sensibilities have elevated the *jhol* to a summer delicacy. With a bit of imagination and culinary flair, the simple *jhol* or stew morphs into a most delicious main course. Ask a Bengali, what he or she would like after a long journey or a week of over indulgence, chances are the answer is *'jhol-bhaat'*.

Jhols or stews can be both vegetarian or non-vegetarian. The star ingredient may be the catch of the day, such as *Rui* (carp), *Magur* (cat fish), *Parshe* (mullet), *Tangra*, *Katla*, *Shinghi* and even *Chingri* (prawn) and *Ilish* (hilsa). Then there is the king of *jhols* – *kochi pathar jhol*. A delicious mild curried stew, of young goat, cooked without garlic or onions, but long simmered over low heat to tenderize the meat and let the juices flow. This delectable broth is recommended to patients for speedy recovery.

On the other hand, the heart of a good vegetarian *jhol*, is the fresh picked vegetables of the season. The simpler the spices, the fresher the pickings, the better the *jhol*. A bowl of *jhol* is best enjoyed with rice, a wedge of lemon and a few raw green chillies.

* *"Rough tummy, tired soul? All weather remedy is the jhol"*

——— RECIPES ———

Garam Kaler Torkarir Jhol (summer vegetable stew) | Serves Six

Ingredients:

Potato – 200 gms

Parval (*Potol*) – 200 gms

Red pumpkin – 200 gms

Brinjal – 200 gms

Ridge gourd – 200 gms

Drumstick – 2 (cut in to 1½" pieces)

Dried lentil ball (*bori*) – 12

Sunflower/ mustard oil – 3 tbsp

Green chilli – 5 (slit and seeded)

Panch phoron – 1 tsp

Salt & sugar – to taste

Method:

Wash, peel and cut all vegetables lengthwise. Heat 1 tbsp oil in a pan, fry dried lentil balls till golden and keep aside. Pour rest of the oil in the pan, heat till it smokes, add *panch phoron* and 2 green chillies, pour all vegetables and drumstick except red pumpkin. Add sugar according to your taste. Fry lightly, then add red pumpkin. Fry for 2 minutes. Pour water, green chillies and salt. Cover and simmer remove cover, add fried *bories*. Cover again boil for another 2 minutes. Remove from fire and serve.

- *Shaak* or spinach, specially the *kalmi* variety added to the *jhol*, makes this summer broth delicious.

Mangshor Jhol (meat stew with spices) | Serves Six

Ingredients:

Meat (goat) – 1 kg (tender)

Potato – 500 gms

Asafoetida – ½ tsp

Aniseed/ fennel – 1 tsp (whole), 1½ tsp (paste)

Turmeric powder/ paste – 3 tsp

Red chilli powder/ paste – 2 tsp

Cumin powder / paste – 3 tsp

Coriander powder/ paste – 2 tsp

Ginger paste – 1 tbsp

Mustard oil – 100 gms

Water – 700 ml (warm)

Salt & sugar – to taste

Method:

Marinate meat with 1 tsp turmeric, ½ tsp chilli, ½ tsp cumin, ½ coriander, ½ tsp ginger with ½ tsp sugar and 1tbsp mustard oil for at least 1 hour. Wash, peel and halve the potatoes, fry lightly and keep aside. Heat rest of the mustard oil in a pan, add asafoetida and whole aniseed, fry. Now put all the remaining spices and sugar, fry. Add marinated meat and fry for 5 minutes in low heat. Put fried potatoes and salt, fry. Now pour warm water, cover the pan with a tight lid, cook till meat is tender .

Alternatively pressure cook.

Morich Jhol (vegetable stew with green chillies)

Serves Six

Ingredients:

Potato – 200 gms
Brinjal – 200 gms
Red pumpkin – 200 gms
Ridge gourd – 200 gms
Horse radish – 2
Spinach/ leafy stems of gourd – a bunch
Green chilli – 8 (whole)
Black peppercorns – 6 (whole)
Onion seed – 1 tsp (whole), 1 tsp paste
Poppy seed – 1 tbsp (grind to paste)
Milk & water – 1 cup each
Sunflower/ mustard oil – 2 tbsp
Salt & sugar – to taste

Method:

Wash, peel and cut all vegetables into cubes. Cut spinach/ leafy stem of gourd into 2 pieces. Now mix poppy and onion seed pastes with milk and keep aside. Heat oil in a pan, add onion seeds, peppercorns and 3-4 green chillies. Fry all vegetables except spinach in low heat for 3 minutes, add spinach, sugar and salt. Pour poppy and onion seed paste dissolved in milk and green chillies. Simmer till vegetables are tender. Add more milk or water, if the gravy is too thick.

🎝

Sheet Kaler Torkarir Jhol (winter vegetable stew)

Serves Six

Ingredients:

Cauliflower – 1 (cut into florets)
Potato – 200 gms
Horse radish – 2 (medium sized)
Tomato – 150 gms
Coriander leaf – 2 tbsp (chopped)
Green chilli – 8 (slit & seeded)
Drumstick – 2 (cut in to 1½" pieces)
Turmeric powder/ paste – ½ tsp
Coriander powder/ paste – ½ tsp
Cumin powder/ paste – ½ tsp
Panch phoron – ½ tsp
Mustard oil – 1 tbsp
Salt – to taste

Method:

Wash, peel and cut all vegetables length-wise. Mix turmeric, coriander and cumin in a bowl with 2 cups of water and salt. Keep aside. Heat oil in a pan, fry *panch phoron* with 2 green chillies. Now put in the vegetables and fry lightly. Pour the liquid spice mixture. Add chillies, cover and simmer till done. Garnish with coriander leaves and serve.

OPTION:

Same method can be used for summer vegetables like parval/ *potol*, brinjals and drumsticks and dried lentil balls (*bori*).

Rui Machher Jhol (fish and vegetable stew)

Ingredients:

Rui/ katla fish – 500 gms

Potato – 200 gms

Parval (potol) – 150 gms

Drumstick – 2 pcs (cut into 2" bits)

Dried lentil ball (*bori*) – 25 gms

Turmeric powder/ paste – 1½ tsp

Red chilli powder/ paste – 1 tsp, 4 (whole)

Dried red chilli – 2 (whole)

Cumin powder/ paste – 1½ tsp

Coriander powder/ paste – 1½ tsp

Mustard oil – 2 tbsp

Panch phoran – 1 tsp

Green chilli – 3 (whole)

Bay leaf – 2 pcs

Salt and sugar – to taste

Method:

Wash, peel and cut potatoes lengthwise. Chop the parval into long halves. Smear fish pieces with turmeric and salt, fry lightly in oil and keep aside. Fry dried lentil balls in the same oil and keep aside. Pour more oil, fry *panch phoran*, whole dried red chillies and bay leaves. Add all vegetables and fry for a minute, put in all spices with a little water along with sugar and fry. Add more water, salt and green chillies, cover the pan and boil until half done. Now put in the fried *bories* and fish, cook till done.

Aamer Jhol (green mangoes in sweet & sour sauce)

Ingredients:

Raw mango – 400 gms

Oil – 1 tbsp

Mustard seed – 1 tsp

Turmeric powder/ paste – ¼ tsp

Sugar – 200 gms

Method:

Peel and slice mangoes. Soak pieces in water for some time.

Fry mustard seeds, and when they splutter, add mango, turmeric and stir. Pour three cups of water and sugar, simmer till the mango is soft. Chill before serving.

Machh

Rakamari Machh

— delicious fish

"In the hands of an expert cook, fish can become an inexhaustible source of perpetual delight"

– Savarin (1755-1826)

There is a quaint wedding custom amongst certain Bengali families. A bride is asked to grip a wriggling *'magur'* (cat fish) when she enters her new home, awfully scary for a new generation bride who may have wanted all the trappings of a traditional Bengali wedding, but did not expect to wrestle with a slithery creature!

What is the significance of this fishy ritual? Is it because the Bay of Bengal is teeming with fish, that the newly-wed has to come to grips with it? In olden days, brides had to learn to cut, dress and cook these live creatures as part of their household duties.

Then there is the wedding trousseau, sent in arrays of trays laden with splendid gifts and amongst it a large and plump *rui* (carp). It is decorated with *sindur* or vermillion and is proudly displayed for all to see and gauge the prosperity and status of the in-law's. The bigger the fish, greater the prestige.

A mother-to-be, weeks before she gives birth, is feted with a platter full of delicacies comprising fish, vegetable preparations and sweets, all her favourite food is carefully prepared and served, but no meat. The carp's head is considered a delicacy and is imperative to this ceremony called, *Shadh*.

Fish features strongly in the lives and culture of Bengalis. Fish features in birth, marriage and death rituals. At a sit down meal after *'niyom bhango'* (end of mourning period), fish is a must, meat is taboo.

Fish is so much a part of life in Bengal, it features in arts and crafts as well. The famous *'Baluchori'* silks of Vishnupur and *Dhaniakhali* and *Tangail* cottons feature fish motifs.

——— FISH, GLORIOUS FISH ———

Some consider hilsa to be the queen of fish. If so, then the carp must be considered the king. And the title of emperor must be bestowed on the Calcutta *bhetki* (Asian seabass). *Bhetki* is unique, its home is the river Hooghly. It lives in fresh waters and breeds in the oceans or estuaries. Its flaky white meat is versatile, sweet and fleshy. There is a tale behind the name of this prized fish. In 19th century Bengal, the fish was offered as a 'bhet' or gift to British dignitaries by merchants and traders to get favours. Thus it was 'bhet-ki' fish, in other words bribe worthy fish!

The most popular variety is *rui* or carp, found in lakes, ponds and fresh water catchments. The *rui* comes in many sizes, from *chara pona* (baby carp) to medium and large, the bigger ones are cut and sold. Every bit of the carp is relished. The heads and tails are considered delicacies. *Katla* is a close relative of the *rui* and is also a fresh water fish. It can be distinguished by its large head. The flesh is pulpy and tasty. And can pass off as *Rui*.

Another prized fish is the *topshe* (mango fish), which breeds in sandy river beds. No bigger than the palm of ones hand, the fish is fried crisply in batter and served on special occasions.

——— FRESH FISH SOLD HERE ———

Bengal is situated in low lying marshy areas, fed by rivers, rivulets, lakes and ponds. It is also near the Bay of Bengal. Canning, a major port, is only about 40 miles from the centre of Kolkata. Trains and trucks laden with the early morning bounties of sea and river arrive daily to the city's markets. Fish, prawns and crabs are bred in *bheris* or artificial tanks. Prawns and crabs are much sought after and the fastidious Bengali will only buy crabs which are alive and kicking! Certain types of fish like the *koi, magur* and *shinghi* (varieties of cat fish) are kept alive in water tanks to ensure maximum freshness. It is not unusual to see these wriggling creatures jump out occasionally and startle the unsuspecting shopper.

> "*In purchasing whole fish, the only way to tell whether it is fresh, is to open the gills and satisfy yourself... they should be moist and bright red and not dry muddy brown*"
> – G. L. Routleff (from an excerpt on British Raj cook book)

——— RECIPES ———

Any type of fish may be substituted for these recipies.

Rui Machher Kalia (fish and potato curry)
| Serves five

Ingredients:

Rui/ katla (carp) – 500 gms

Potato – 250 gms

Onion chopped – ½ cup

Onion paste – 1½ tbsp

Ginger paste – 1 tsp

Red chilli powder/ paste – 1 tsp

Turmeric powder/ paste – 1 tsps

Mustard oil – 150 gms

Bay leaf – 2

Green cardamom – 3

Cloves – 4

Cinnamon stick – 2 inch

Salt & sugar – to taste

Method:

Wash, peel and cut potatoes lengthwise into 4 pieces. Smear fish pieces with turmeric and salt, fry lightly in oil and keep aside. Pour more oil and heat on a high flame. Fry bay leaves, green cardamom, cloves and cinnamon. Add chopped onions, fry till brown, then add onion and ginger pastes, fry for 2 minutes. Put in potatoes and fry for another two minutes. Add red chillies with sugar and salt, fry well. Pour water, cover and boil. When potatoes are tender and the gravy thickens slightly, put in fried fish and cook until done.

Rui Machher Korma (rich fish curry)
| Serves five

Ingredients:

Rui (carp) – 500 gms

Onion paste – 2 tbsp (large)

Garlic paste – 1 tsp

Ginger paste – 1½ tsp

Turmeric powder/ paste – 1½ tsp

Mustard oil – 150 gms

Whole cinnamon, cloves and cardamoms for tempering

Red chilli powder/ paste – 2 tsp

Yoghurt – 3 tbsp (beaten)

Salt & sugar – to taste

Method:

Smear fish pieces with turmeric and salt, fry lightly in oil and set aside.

In the same oil, add whole cinnamon, cloves and cardamoms.

When a spicy aroma floats up, add onion, garlic and ginger. Gently fry.

Add turmeric and chilli. Fry again. Add yoghurt, salt and sugar, fry well. Then add water. Let the gravy come to a boil, put in fish.

Cook till the gravy thickens.

Doi Machh (fish with yoghurt)

Ingredients:

Rui/ katla (carp) – 500 gms (cut into large pieces)
Onion paste – 5 tbsp
Ginger paste – 2 tbsp
Turmeric powder/ paste – 1½ tsp
Yoghurt – 250 gms (beaten)
Cardamom – 8 & Cinnamon stick – 6
Mustard oil – 2 tbsp
Bay leaf – 2
Green chilli – 10 (slit)
Ghee – 1 tbsp
Salt & sugar – to taste

Method:

Marinate the fish in salt, turmeric, some of the yoghurt and half the onion and ginger pastes for two hours. Powder half the cardamoms and cinnamon sticks.

In hot oil, add bay leaves, remaining cardamoms and cinnamon sticks. Add remaining onion and ginger pastes, stir.

Pour in the remaining yoghurt (beaten well with sugar) and stir again. Add 2 cups of water, when it comes to a boil, put in the fish and green chillies. When the fish is cooked, add ghee, cardamom-cinnamon powder and remove from fire.

Bhetki Machher Paturi (fish in plantain leaves)

Ingredients:

Bhetki (beckti) – 500 gms (pieces)
Mustard seed – 25 gms
White mustard seed – 25 gms
Mustard oil – ¼ cup
Turmeric powder/ paste – 1 tsp
Green chilli – 2
Plantain leaves
Thread/ string to tie-up
Salt & sugar – to taste

(Optional: coconut paste, in which case reduce the quantity of mustard).

Cook *hilsa, koi* fish or prawns in the same manner.

Method:

Make pastes from two kinds of mustard seeds with salt and a green chillies. Marinate fish in the mustard paste, oil, turmeric, salt, sugar and green chillies (also coconut paste – optional) for half an hour. Cut plantain leaves into rectangles. There should be two rectangles per piece of fish.

Place a piece of marinated fish on plantain leaf. Fold the corners to form an envelope and tie with thread. Do the same with all fish pieces. Now cook envelopes on a griddle over a low flame till envelopes turns brown. *Paturi* is served with the fish inside the envelope. The packets can be steamed as well.

Chital Machher Muitha (fish ball curry) | Serves five

Ingredients:

Chital (clown knife fish) – 500 gms

Potato – 200 gms (boiled and mashed)

Turmeric powder/ paste – 2 tsp

Dried red chilli powder/ paste – 1½ tsp

Garam masala powder/ paste – 2 tsp

Ginger paste – 3 tsp

Mustard oil – 125 gms

Bay leaf – 3

Cumin seed – 1 tsp

Onion paste – 2 tbsp

Garlic paste – ½ tsp

Cumin powder/ paste – 1 tsp

Ghee – 1 tsp

Salt – to taste

Method:

Scrape flesh from fish with the help of a spoon. Hold up the fish by the tail with one hand and use the spoon in the other. Combine the flesh with mashed potato, salt, half the turmeric and *garam masala*, ½ tsp chilli, 1 tsp ginger. Mix well.

Boil water in a pot. Make large balls (dumplings) with fish mixture and drop these into boiling water. Remove balls once they harden, drain, cool and cut into small chunks.

Fry fish chunks till golden and keep aside.

In another pan fry red chillies and cumin seeds, onion and garlic pastes, remaining ginger and turmeric pastes, cumin and chilli pastes and salt, add water and stir well. Now add fish and water if required.

When the gravy thickens, top with *garam masala* and ghee. Remove from fire.

——— CHHOTO MACHH ———

small fish, big delight

The rivers and ponds of Bengal yield a variety of sprats and small fish. These can be cooked to stretch and feed many mouths. Bengalis simply delight in the small varieties of fish because they are lip-smacking delicious.

Like the white bait or herrings in the west, most of these fish are consumed whole with the head and tail intact. Only the scales are removed, slit and gutted before cooking. The minnows and tiny ones are merely washed, scrubbed clean and cooked. Curried or fried, small fish are delicious and nutritious.

Parshey Machher Jhol Begun Diye (stewed fish with brinjals)

Ingredients: | **Method:** | Serves four

Parshey (mullet) – 8 (medium)

Brinjal – 2 (medium sized)

Turmeric powder/ paste – 2 tsp

Red chilli powder/ paste – 1 tsp

Coriander leaf – 2 tbsp (chopped)

Onion Seed – 1 tsp

Green chilli – 6 (slit)

Mustard oil – 2 tbsp

Salt – To taste

Method: Serves four

Cut brinjals lengthwise into 8 pieces. Coat mullet with a pinch of turmeric and salt. Heat 1 tbsp mustard oil in a pan and fry the fish lightly, remove and drain. Add onion seeds and two green chillies in same oil, add brinjal pieces, fry lightly. Mix turmeric and chilli in a cup of water and pour into pan. Bring to boil, add fried fish, green chillies and salt. Simmer till done. Garnish with mustard oil and coriander leaves. Serve hot.

Kajli Machher Jhol (spicy sprats)

Serves four

Ingredients:

Kajli (gangetic ailia) – 500 gms

Turmeric powder/ paste – 1 ½ tsp

Onion seed – 1 tsp

Coriander powder/ paste – 1 tsp

Cumin powder/ paste – 1 tsp

Red chilli powder/ paste – 1 tsp

Green chilli – 6

Mustard oil – 2 tbsp

Coriander leaf – 1 (small bunch)

Salt – to taste

Method:

Smear fish with salt and turmeric. Fry fish lightly and carefully, drain and keep aside. Add onion seeds and a two green chillies in heated oil. Fry till they splutter. Mix all other spices in ½ cup of water and pour into the oil and stir. When water comes to a boil, add fried fish and salt, simmer for few minutes. Add remaining green chillies. Cook till done. Garnish with coriander leaves and serve.

Kajli fish breaks easily, so avoid stirring too much or over cooking.

Shorshe Pabda (fish in mustard gravy)
Serves four

Ingredients:

Pabda (Indian butter fish) – 8 (medium)

Dried lentil ball (*bori*) – 12

Onion seed – 1 tsp

Turmeric powder/ paste – ½ tsp

Green chilli – 6 (slit)

Mustard paste – 5 tsp

Mustard oil – 2 tbsp

Coriander leaf – 1 tbsp (chopped)

Salt – to taste

Method:

Smear fish with salt and turmeric. Fry dried lentil balls and fish separately, drain and keep aside. In the same pan, fry onion seeds and two green chillies, add salt, turmeric and mustard pastes dissolved in a cup of water, bring to boil. Put in the lentil balls, simmer. When gravy begins to thicken, add fish one at a time. Gently turn the fish and cook till done. Garnish with coriander leaves before serving.

Bele Machher Jhuri (stir fried fish flakes)
Serves four

Ingredients:

Bele machh (tank Goby) – 500 gms

Turmeric powder/ paste – 1 tsp

Mustard oil – 50 gms

Onion – 200 gms (chopped)

Ginger – 1" (chopped)

Green chilli – 2 (chopped)

Salt – To taste

Method:

Remove fish heads and tails and cut each fish into three pieces. Boil fish lightly and take out bones. Shred fish and mix with salt and turmeric. In hot oil fry chopped onions, ginger and green chillies till golden then add fish and salt, fry well. Garnish with chillies.

Kachki Machher Charchchari (stir fried sprats)
Serves four

Ingredients:

Kachki (sprat) – 500 gms

Turmeric powder/ paste – 1 tsp

Onion – 1 tbsp (paste), 2 (chopped)

Garlic powder/ paste – ½ tsp

Green chilli – 1 tsp (paste) & 3 (whole)

Mustard oil – 3 tbsp

Salt – to taste

Method:

Smear fish with salt, turmeric, onion, garlic and green chilli pastes.

Fry chopped onions add fish, green chillies and salt, fry well. Stir gently or the fish will break.

Cook till oil floats to the top.

Tangrar Jhal (spicy cat fish)

Serves four

Ingredients:

Tangra (cat fish) – 8 (mediun sized)
Onion – 200 gms (chopped)
Ginger paste – ½ tsp
Turmeric powder/ paste – 1 tsp
Red chilli powder/ paste – 1 tsp
Cumin powder/ paste – 1 tsp
Mustard oil – 100 gms
Green chilli – 6 (slit)
Cinnamon stick – 2"
Clove – 4
Cardamom – 4
Salt – to taste

Method:

Smear fish with a pinch of salt and turmeric. Fry fish, drain and keep aside.

Fry cinnamon, cloves, cardamoms, and chopped onions. Add ginger, red chilli, cumin and fry well. Add ½ cup of water and simmer, then add fish one at a time in the gravy with, green chillies and salt. Cook till gravy thickens.

> *Pabda* (Indian butter fish) can be cooked in the same way.

Mourala Machher Tauk (tiny fish in sweet-sour gravy)

Serves four

Ingredients:

Mourala (mola carplet) – 300 gms
Turmeric powder/ paste – ¼ tsp
Dried red chilli – 2 (whole)
Mustard seed – ¼ tsp
Tamarind pulp – 3 tbsp
Jaggery/ molasses – 50 gms
Mustard oil – 2 tbsp
Salt – to taste

Method:

Fry fish in hot oil till crisp, remove from fire. In a fresh pan heat 1 tbsp oil and put in dried red chillies and mustard seeds. When mustard seeds splutter, add tamarind pulp mixed with water, salt and turmeric. When the gravy comes to a boil, add jaggery, stir to dissolve it well. Lastly, add fish and simmer.

The gravy should be like a stew.

Gurjali Machher Jhaal (sea fish curry)

Ingredients:

Gurjali (Indian salmon) – 8 whole if medium sized/ chunky pieces, if large)

Turmeric paste/ powder – as needed

Dried red chilli – 2 (whole), 1 tbsp (powder)

Onion paste – 2 tbsp

Garlic paste – 2 tsp

Coriander powder/ paste – 1 tbsp

Cumin powder/ paste – 1 tbsp

Garam masala powder/ paste – 1 tbsp

Cinnamon – 2"

Cloves – 4

Cardamom – 2 whole

Tomato –1 (chopped)

Green chilli – 4

Mustard oil – 3 tbsp

Coriander leaves – 1 bunch (chopped)

Salt – to taste

Method:

Smear fish with salt and turmeric. If whole, clean and de-scale. Fry fish. Set aside. Fry whole red chillies, cloves, cardamoms and cinnamon. Fry all other ingredients well with tomatoes. When well done, add fish, green chillies and salt. Cover and simmer. Add water, turn the fish. Garnish with coriander leaves. Fresh coconut milk can be used instead of water.

An alternative recipe:

Fry fish, keep aside. Heat oil, fry one teaspoon of *panch phoron,* add chopped onions, garlic and tomatoes, fry well. Add water, cover and cook to make a thick gravy. Add fish. When done, garnish with coriander leaves.

> Any other sea fish like Mackerel, Pomfret or Sardines can be used for the recipe above.

Tel Koi (fish in mustard oil)

Ingredients:

Koi (climbing perch) – 6 (large)

Turmeric powder/ paste – 1 ½ tsp

Onion seed – 4 ½ tsp

Mustard oil – 6 tbsp

Green chilli – 6 to 8

Salt – to taste

Method:

Smear fish with salt and turmeric, fry lightly and keep aside. Grind four tsp onion seeds with one green chilli to make a paste. Heat half of the remaining oil, put ½ tsp onion seeds and two green chillies and fry. Add salt, turmeric dissolved in a cup of water and simmer. Put in the fried fish. Cook till half done, now add the onion seed paste, salt and green chillies, cook till done. Top with one teaspoon of mustard oil.

Machher Dom (fish with spice and yoghurt)

| Serves four

Ingredients:

Fish – 8 pieces (large)

Onion – 2 tbsp (chopped), 4 tbsp (paste)

Garlic – 2 tsp (chopped), 1 tbsp (paste)

Ginger paste – 1 tbsp

Yoghurt – 200 gms (beaten)

Turmeric powder/ paste – 1 ½ tsp

Chilli powder/ paste – 2 tsp

Cardamom & clove – 6 each (whole)

Cinnamon stick – 4 (1 inch pieces)

Bay leaf – 2

Green chilli – 4 (slit & seeded)

Mustard oil – 2 tbsp

Salt & sugar – to taste

Method:

Marinate fish with turmeric, chilli, garlic, ginger, onion paste and yoghurt with salt, sugar and little oil for 30 minutes. Heat remaining oil in a pan, add bay leaves, cloves, cardamoms, cinnamon and fry well. Add chopped garlic and onions, fry till golden brown. Now pour marinated fish with the mixture and green chillies. Cover tightly and cook in low heat till done.

Remove from fire. Serve hot.

> Can be cooked with any big fish like carp, beckti or cat fish

---

Koi Machher Hara Parbati (spicy two-in-one fish curry)

| Serves four

Ingredients:

Koi (climbing perch) – 8 (large)

Turmeric powder/ paste – 1 tsp

Mustard oil – 4 tbsp

Mustard paste – 1½ tbsp

Green chilli paste – 3 tsp

Dried red chilli powder/ paste – 1 tsp

Tamarind paste – 1½ tbsp

Salt & sugar – to taste

> Hara is Lord Shiva, Parbati is his wife

Method:

Smear fish with salt and turmeric, fry and keep aside. Heat oil in a pan, mix mustard, half the green chilli paste, red chilli powder, salt and three spoons of water and fry well. In another pan heat remaining oil, mix tamarind paste, green chilli paste, red chilli powder, sugar and water. Boil till the gravy thickens. Now you have two distinct gravies, one with a mustard flavour, and other with a sweet and sour taste. Smear the mustard gravy on one side of the fried fish and other side with tamarind gravy. This fish preparation has a unique two-in-one flavour.

Alu-phulkopi Diye Bhetki Machh

| Serves four

(fish curry with potato, tomato and cauliflower)

Ingredients:

Bhetki (beckti) – 500 gms (large pieces)

Potato – 200 gms

Cauliflower – 1 (medium sized)

Tomato – 150 gms

Bay leaf – 2 pcs

Dried red chilli – 2 (whole)

Green cardamom – 4

Clove – 4

Cinnamon – 2 inch

Onion paste – 2 tbsp

Ginger paste – 1tbsp

Turmeric powder/ paste – 1 tsp

Red chilli powder/ paste – 1 tsp

Green chilli – 2 (slit and seeded)

Mustard oil –150 gms

Coriander leaves – 2 tbsp (chopped)

Salt & sugar – to taste

Method:

Wash, peel and cut potatoes lengthwise. Wash cauliflower and cut into florets. Smear fish pieces with turmeric and salt, fry lightly. Now, fry cauliflowers and potatoes lightly and separately and keep aside.

Heat oil in pan, add bay leaves, dried red chilli, cardamoms, cloves and cinnamon, fry well. Put onion paste and fry, add chopped tomatoes, turmeric, chilli powder and ginger, fry well. Add fried cauliflowers and potatoes with sugar, fry in low heat. Add two cups of water, salt and green chillies, cook till tender. Now add fried fish, cook till done. Garnish with chopped coriander leaves. Serve with rice.

> In winter, fresh green peas can be added.

Tips:

- Rub hands in sour curd or vinegar or a lemon juice and sugar to get relief from itching after grinding or chopping chillies.

- To remove the smell of onions or fish from hands rub with a mixture of coffee and water.

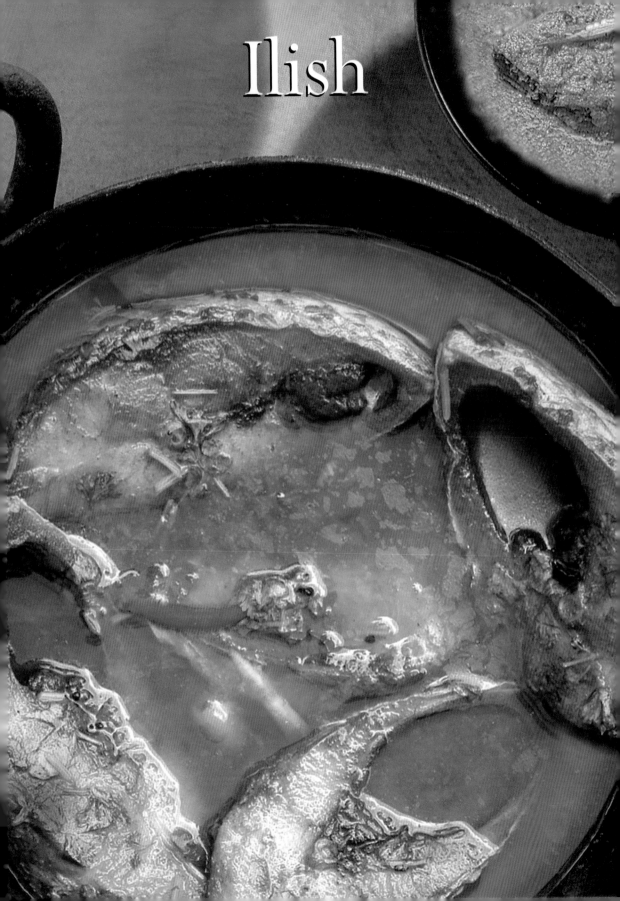

Ilish

Machher Rani

— queen of fish

"Ilshe guri, ilshe guri ilish machher dim..." *
— a popular Bengali rhyme

Hilsa, a seasonal delicacy is absolutely heavenly to eat! It surfaces in markets when the monsoon arrives in Bengal in July or August and disappears with the first whiff of winter winds. The hilsa is considered the queen of all fish.

Bengalis are proud of several gastronomic features unique to this state. Topping the list are Darjeeling tea and the hilsa. Both are considered exquisite in terms of flavour and taste. We will talk of tea later but first the epicurean delight of the muddy waters of Ganges.

Why is the hilsa so special? This delicious and elusive creature has a rare character. It is not only ephemeral, its silvery scales and elegant tapering shape conceals flesh that is flaky , succulent, imbued with fatty omega oils and a rich taste that is irresistible. When fried it exudes a tempting aroma which can drive Bengalis to frenzy! On the other hand the hilsa has plenty of fine and delicate bones, making it impossible for the uninitiated to eat it without the aid of fingers and gastronomic gumption.

Perhaps this is the reason why trendy restaurants are concocting new ways of cooking this lovely fish. We hasten here to caution the reader to shun these new avatars... the roasts, chutneys, Chinese chilly hilsa and most definitely, the previously unheard of hilsa mousse!! Modern creative distortions are unnecessary and to our mind sacrilegious! In fact most Bengali gourmets would shun the strange discoveries and opt for the traditional recipes, which allow one to relish the *Ilish* (Bengali name) to the last chewable bone and enjoy it to the utmost.

* "Hilsa drops, rain drops. Hilsa is ripe with roe drops"

Coming back to the reason why the *Ilish* is so special. The reason being that hilsa or *Ilish* is a prized and seasonal delicacy which is fished out from the murky waters of the Ganges during the heavy rains. The hilsa's natural habitat lies in the depths of the Bay of Bengal. A sea fish, the hilsa swims to the big muddy rivers through estuaries flowing into the bay, to spawn and release baby hilsas. In winter the hilsa returns to the sea. The western name for this elusive and delicious fish is shad. It is also found in the rivers of South East Asia, like the Yangtse and Irawaddy which flow into the southern sea of this region.

Here are a few tips for the uninitiated:

- The hilsa or *Ilish* is best eaten during the monsoons and eating it after Durga Puja is absolutely taboo perhaps because that's the time when the fish are very, very young.

- The fatter the hilsa better it tastes.

- Hilsa roe is delicious, but the presence of roe in hilsa, does take away the robust, well rounded taste of this oily fish.

- Ideally, hilsa tastes best when cooked in mustard oil – but any white oil will do – ghee is not recommended.

- If you buy a whole fish, ask the seller to cut it for you. If you can bear to watch you'll notice how it is done. First the head comes off, than the scales are expertly erased by a *'bonti'*, or a knife, then the fish is held firmly by both hands and dissected in the middle and made into two halves. Next each half is cut in the middle, the solid triangles are called *'gada'*, the triangles with the hole or roes lodged in between are called *'petis'*.

- The pieces with the 'holes' in the middle are more oily but have less bones.

- If you are a new hilsa eater – we suggest do not attempt to eat the head or tail to avoid disastrous trips to the E.N.T. specialist. And do use your fingers!

- The best accompaniment with hilsa is plain boiled rice.

- Fish heads are used to make delectable charchcharis, chanchras – which are in essence a potpourri of summer vegetables, dominated by the *Pui* variety of spinach which grow profusely in the plains of Bengal.

- *'Tauk or Ambol'* is a sweet and sour broth, a concoction of hilsa heads, a clever and tasty way of disposing the leftovers of the fish. And also making the fish go a long way for larger households.

I am a great hilsa fan, the 'queen of fish' is undoubtedly my favourite. However despite the huge collection of recipes we have gathered, I would like to share a secret. The way I like to eat this fish and the roe is very simple and does not require a recipe at all. Just smear the pieces with a bit of salt and turmeric (*halud*) fry them in smoking mustard oil, gently turn them now and then to get them evenly golden brown, (this way the excess oil seeps out, which many like to savour with boiled rice) then eat the fish with plain steamed rice and a sharp green chilly. If you find this too dry you could spoon a dollop of *mushur daal* to the rice. Delicious!

———— RECIPES ————

Shorse Ilish Begun Diye (hilsa with mustard and brinjal)

Serves four

Ingredients:

Hilsa – 8 pieces

Brinjal – 2 (medium sized)

Turmeric powder/ paste – 1 ½ tsp

Mustard seed – 50 gms

Green chilli – 6 (slit)

Panch phoron – ½ tsp

Mustard oil – 2 tbsp

Salt – to taste

Method:

Cut brinjals lengthwise into 8 pieces. Grind mustard seeds into a paste together with a pinch of salt and a green chilli.

Smear hilsa with turmeric and a pinch of salt.

Heat 1½ tbsp mustard oil in a pan and fry hilsa lightly, drain and keep aside. Add *panch phoron* in hot oil, then add brinjal pieces, fry lightly. Add mixture of mustard and turmeric dissolved in 1½ cups of water into the pan. Boil the mixture, put in fried hilsa pieces, green chilli and salt. Simmer till done. Top with mustard oil. Serve with rice.

OPTION:

This dish can also be made with potatoes, parvals and drum sticks. An interesting summer variation is to add thin slices of green mangoes to make a tangy broth.

Ilish Machher Kancha Jhol (stewed hilsa)

Ingredients:

Hilsa – 8 pieces

Turmeric powder/ paste – 2 tsp

Onion Seed – ½ tsp

Green chilli – 6 (slit)

Mustard oil – 2 tbsp

Salt – to taste

Method:

Coat hilsa with little bit of turmeric and a pinch of salt.

Heat 1½ table spoon of mustard oil in a pan, add onion seeds. Mix the turmeric in a cup of water and pour in to the pan. Bring to boil, add hilsa, green chillies and salt. Simmer till done. Top with rest of the mustard oil. Serve hot.

Doi Ilish (yoghurt hilsa)

Ingredients:

Hilsa – 8 pieces

Yoghurt – 250 gms

Ginger paste – 2 tsp

Turmeric powder/ paste– 1 tsp

Lemon juice – ½ tsp

Mustard seed – ½ tsp

Groundnut oil – 2 tbsp

Green chilli – 4 (slit) and one finely slit

Salt & sugar – to taste

Method:

Coat hilsa with a little bit of turmeric, a pinch of salt and lemon juice.

Beat yoghurt with ginger, sugar, oil and salt. Smear fish with this mixture and add whole green chillies. Place fish mixture in a bowl, cover tightly with a lid, place the bowl in a large pan filled half with water. Cook fish for 10 minutes. Garnish with green chillies and serve.

OPTION:

This preparation can also be cooked in microwave oven.

Tips: All stems, roots and stalks have to be carefully washed and scraped before sizing them for the dish to be prepared.

Ilish Machher Moulo (hilsa in coconut milk)

Ingredients:

Hilsa – 8 pieces

Onion – 100 gms (finely chopped)

Ginger – 1" (finely chopped)

Coconut (fresh) – 1 full (grated)

Red chilli paste/ powder – ½ tsp

Turmeric paste/ powder – ¼ tsp

Green chilli – 5 (finely slit)

Groundnut oil/ mustard oil – 2 tbsp

Coriander leaf – 2 tsp (chopped)

Salt – to taste

Method:

Smear hilsa with turmeric and salt. Fry lightly. Soak grated coconut in 1½ cups of hot water, keep it for five minutes. Squeeze coconut well to extract milk.

In a pan heat rest of the oil and fry chopped onions till brown, add coconut milk, boil for one minute, add ginger, red chilli powder, coriander leaves and green chillies, simmer, add hilsa and simmer till done.

Ilish Paturi (hilsa in pumpkin leaves)

Ingredients:

Hilsa – 8 pieces

Turmeric powder/ paste – 1 ½ tsp

Mustard seed – 100 gms

Green chilli – 3

Mustard oil – 3 tbsp

Salt – to taste

Pumpkin leaf – 8 (large)

String/ thread

Method:

Grind mustard seeds with green chillies to make a paste. Mix all ingredients with hilsa pieces and season for 15 minutes. Wash pumpkin leaves and drain. Take one pumpkin leaf for one piece of hilsa. Place seasoned hilsa piece at the centre of each leaf, fold to cover and tie with thread. Fry all pumpkin leaf envelopes in a flat bottomed pan or tawa, in low heat. Remove thread at the time of serving. The fish is to be eaten with the leaves.

Ilish Bhape (steamed hilsa in mustard gravy)

Ingredients:

Hilsa – 8 pieces

Turmeric powder/ paste – 2 tsps

Red chilli powder/ paste – 1 tsp

Mustard seed – 100 gms

Mustard oil – 75 gms

Green chilli – 8 (slit & seeded)

Salt – to taste

Method:

Grind mustard seeds into a paste with a pinch of salt and 2 green chillies.

Mix hilsa pieces with mustard paste, turmeric, red chillies, salt, green chillies and mustard oil.

Put this mixture in a bowl with a tight lid, place the bowl in a large pan filled with water, care should be taken so that water level does not exceed more than one third of the bowl. Put pan on fire, bring to boil, simmer for 30 minutes.

OPTION:

This preparation can also be cooked in microwave oven.

Kanchakoladiye Ilish Machh (hilsa stew with raw banana)

Ingredients:

Hilsa – 8 pieces

Raw banana – 2

Turmeric powder/ paste – 2 tsp

Onion seed – 2 tsp

Green chilli paste – 1 tbsp

Green chilli – 8 (slit & seeded)

Mustard oil – 75 gms

Salt – to taste

Method:

Wash, peel and cut raw banana into one and half inch size pieces like fingers. Mix turmeric and salt in a bowl with water and keep aside. Heat oil in a pan (keep 1 tbsp of oil aside), put onion seeds and two green chillies, add banana pieces and fry till golden. Pour turmeric-salt mix, cover and cook till banana pieces are half done. Now add hilsa pieces with green chillies and cook till done. Remove from fire and add raw mustard oil. Serve hot with rice.

Tips: Wrap ripe bananas with a wet muslin cloth and put in the refrigerator to prevent them from getting black. The bananas will remain fresh for a week.

Ilish Machher Tauk (piquant hilsa)

Ingredients:

Hilsa – 4 pieces

Tamarind pulp – 2 tsp

Panch phoron – ½ teaspoon

Dried red chilli – 2 (whole)

Turmeric powder/ paste – ½ teaspoon

Mustard paste – 1 table spoon

Sugar – 1 tea spoon (more if required)

Green chilli – 4 whole (slited)

Mustard oil – 2 tsp

Salt – to taste

Method:

In a cup of water add tamarind, leave for 5 minutes. Stir well with a spoon to mix tamarind evenly with water.

Smear hilsa with turmeric and salt. Keep aside. Heat oil in a pan, add dry red chilli, and *panch phoron*, cook till spices stop spluttering. Add hilsa and fry. Pour tamarind juice with one cup of water. Bring to boil, add sugar, salt and green chilli, boil for 1 minute, add mustard paste, simmer for 2 minutes.

◆◆

HILSA

Scientific Name: *Tenualosa ilisha*

Commonly called: Hilsa/ *Ilish*

Distribution: Indian Ocean – Persian Gulf eastward to Myanmar, including western and eastern coast of India. Anadromous in nature (a phenomenon in tropical water), schooling in coastal waters and migrates up to 1200 Km in land through rivers.

Standard length: 36 cm – 42 cm, maximum length recorded: 60 cm

Standard weight: 680 gm to 1300 gm. Maximum weight recorded 2490 gm.

Mangsho

Mukhorochok Mangsho
– mouthwatering meat

"They had a cook with them who stood alone.
For boiling chicken with marrow and bone
Sharp flavouring powder and a spice to savour..."
— Geoffrey Chaucer

For many Bengalis, a classic spicy, red meat curry is a special treat. It breaks the monotony of the daily rice and fish routine, and is considered an extravagant addition to the menu, a welcome meatiness that adds zing at weddings, religious festivals or at any gathering for that matter. When thinking up a suitably impressive menu for a dinner party, the Bengali hostess will often turn to the tried-and-tested meat curry-rice option that, no matter how often it puts in an appearance at the table, never fails to please. A really well-cooked, authentic meat curry in the traditional Bengali style has a distinctive flavour and fragrance, hard to replicate, which every Bengali knows and recognizes, is almost guaranteed to get the taste buds salivating in advance.

There are variations on how a meat curry can be cooked: from the *jhol* or stew which offers up a light fresh tomato and turmeric-based gravy excellent for soaking up a mound of steamed rice, to a rich, oily Mughal-inspired *rezala* redolent of cloves and cinnamon that goes well with flatbread like *parathas*, or the drier, well-stirred onion-based *kasha* which goes down beautifully with a stack of hot, fresh *rotis* and a crisp salad on the side. Almost as versatile as the ubiquitous fish, meat is intrinsic to the entire Bengali food experience.

———— RECIPES ————

Mangshor Kalia (rich meat curry)

Ingredients:

Meat – 600 gms (tender goat meat)
Potato – 4 (halved)
Onion – 3 tbsp (paste), 2 (chopped)
Ginger paste – 1 tbsp
Garlic paste – 1 tsp
Turmeric powder/ paste – 1 tsp
Chilli powder/ paste – 1 tsp
Coriander powder/ paste – 1 ½ tsp
Cumin powder/ paste – 1 tsp
Yoghurt – 100 gms
Mustard oil – 100 gms
Ghee – 1tbsp
Bay leaf – 4
Garam masala powder/ paste –1 tsp
Salt – to taste

Method:

Marinate meat in onion, ginger, garlic, turmeric, coriander, cumin and chilli paste with yoghurt and 25 gms of mustard oil for about an hour.

Heat rest of the mustard oil. Fry potatoes lightly and keep aside. In the same oil put bay leaves, chopped onions, and fry till onions are golden. Add the marinated meat and fry well. The meat will release its juices. Cook till dry. Add hot water and salt cover and cook. When meat is half done add potatoes and cook till done. Top with *garam masala* and ghee. Serve hot

———— ⬭ ————

Kasha Mangsho (dry and spicy meat curry)

Ingredients:

Meat – 1 kg
Onion – 500 gms (chopped)
Kashmir red chilli powder/ paste – 4 tsp
Garam masala powder/ paste – 2 tsp
Yoghurt – 300 gms (beaten)
Ginger paste – 1 ½ tbsp
Garlic paste – 1 tbsp
Mustard oil – 150 gms
Salt – to taste

Method:

Heat mustard oil in a heavy bottomed pan and fry onions till well browned. Add meat, chilli, ginger and garlic pastes and salt. Fry well. Add yoghurt and fry again. Pour a cup of hot water, cover and simmer for some time, stirring and sprinkling water occasionally to ensure that the gravy does not stick to the bottom of the pan. When meat is tender and the gravy is thick, sprinkle *garam masala* paste and remove from fire.

Mangshor Korma (exotic meat curry) | Serves four

Ingredients:

Chicken or meat – 1 kg

Onion – 6 large (chopped)

Yoghurt – 1½ cups

Ginger paste – 2 ½ tbsp

Garlic paste – 4 tbsp (3 tbsp for chicken)

Coriander powder/ paste – 2 tbsp

Chilli powder/ paste – 1 ½ tbsp (optional)

Garam masala powder/ paste –1 tbsp

Mustard oil – 150 gms

Salt & sugar – to taste

Method:

Marinate meat in a mixture of yoghurt and ginger, garlic, coriander and chilli pastes for two hours. Heat 100 gms oil in a pan and fry onions till brown and crisp and keep aside. Add rest of the oil in the pan, heat and put in marinated meat and fry. When meat releases its juices, cover and cook on a low flame till meat is half done. Next, remove lid and fry on medium heat, adding salt and sugar. When meat is tender and gravy is thick, add *garam masala* paste and fried onions. Remove from fire.

- If chicken is used, it should become tender in the process of frying. Meat will have to be cooked covered for a longer period, with more water, added if necessary.

Mangshor Tauk Jhal (hot and sour meat curry) | Serves four

Ingredients:

Meat – 1 kg

Cumin seed – 2 tsp

Mustard seed – 1 tsp

Turmeric powder/ paste – 1tsp

Onion – 3 (large) sliced

Ginger paste – 1 tsp

Garlic – 10 cloves

Dry red chilli – 5

Peppercorn – 1 tbsp (whole)

Cinnamon – 2 pcs (1"each)

Clove – 8

Cardamom (black) – 8

Vinegar – ¾th cups

Mustard oil – 150 gms

Salt & sugar – to taste

Method:

Cut meat into medium sized cubes. Keep aside oil, salt, onions and 2 spoons of vinegar. Grind to a paste all other ingredients with vinegar. Marinate meat well with the paste for 4 hours. Put oil in a pan, heat and fry sliced onions. When onions are soft, add the marinated meat and fry well.

Add salt and rest of the vinegar. Cover pan with lid and cook till oil floats up. Serve hot with rice.

Steamer Curry

| Serves four

In the 1950's a delicious curry used to be served on board the steamer which ferried passengers from *Moniharighat* to *Sakrikalighat* on their journey to Siliguri and Darjeeling. The taste and flavour lingered in my senses. The recipe has been created from memory and experiments.

Ingredients:

Country chicken – 1 kg (cut into pieces)

Cumin powder/ paste – 1 tsp

Coriander powder/ paste – 2 tsp

Ginger/ garlic paste – 1 tbsp

Onion – 2 tbsp (chopped)

Bay leaf – 2

Cinnamon – ½ stick

Clove – 3 or 4

Black cardamom – 1

Red chilli powder – ½ tsp

Red lentil (*mushur daal*) – ½ cup (boiled and strained)

Black pepper powder – a pinch

Mustard oil – 100 gms

Salt – to taste

Method:

Heat oil in a pan. Fry chopped onions, ginger/ garlic pastes, cumin, coriander powder and bay leaves. Add chicken. Fry and add the boiled and strained red lentils to the pot. Boil the chicken with the *daal*. Add more hot water if a thinner gravy is required. Add salt, pepper, cinnamon, cardamom and clove. Simmer in low heat. Serve hot rice and hot pickles or mango chutney.

Tips:

• To get rid of the overpowering smell of turmeric, heat a stone pestle or grinding stone (*nora*) and dip it in the curry for a few minutes.

• To get rid of the smell of onion from your hands rub with mustard oil and salt.

Chingri, Kankra & Dim

Chingri O Kankra
– shell fish pleasures

"We went to Digha, it certainly was the seaside;
For the next, the most blessed of morns,
I remember how fondly I gazed at my bride
Sitting down to a plate full of prawns"

– with apologies to Thomas Hood

Shell fish and crustaceans are particular favourites of the fish loving Bengalis. On special occasions, Bengalis can pay exorbitant prices for the succulent and fresh lobsters actually crayfish, (*galda chingri*) or the much sought after *Bagda*s (prawns). Kolkata is fortunate to have a choice of crabs, prawns and shrimps, not so much because of the rivers, ponds and tanks in the surrounding rural districts but because of the large fisheries that supply the markets all over the city.

When on the subject of prawns and crayfish (*galda chingri*), the reader has to be appraised of the Bengali sensibilities. There is a great divide between those Bengalis who have roots in former East Bengal now Bangladesh and those 'Bongs' whose ancestors always belonged to West Bengal. Today, North Calcutta is generally regarded as their territory. The East Bengalis, now mostly in South Calcutta claim that hilsa is the queen of fish, while the West Bengalis declare *galda chingri* as the gourmet's choice. The war of choices is evident even in the football field. 'Mohon Bagan' signifies West Bengal, and 'East Bengal' is their rival team. Mock fights spill into the fish stalls, the jocular remarks such as "Today put your money on 'Mohun Bagan' brother" as the fish seller points to the large and wiggling crayfish. He shouts "East Bengal has lost!" It is indeed a sensitive issue, which scores over the other.

Incidentally on a visit to Kolkata's posh restaurants one may come across items such as "Lobster Thermidor" or "Lobster Newburg" on the menu. The preparations may or may not be authentic, but the shell fish is most likely to be crayfish not lobster.

The bazaars or fish markets display a bedazzling array. The vociferous cries of fish mongers vie with each other to call and 'catch' the well heeled customer. Voices rise and shouts are as descriptive as they are sometimes humorous. Once, when asked whether the crabs had eggs, the fish monger answered rather coyly that he was not aware whether the crab had engaged in any lascivious activities underwater! In other words he could not guarantee crabs eggs by the look of the crustacean.

Tiger prawns, wriggling shrimps, blue shelled prawns, fresh crayfish with wiggly claws and a huge variety of baby shrimps lie temptingly on blocks of ice. The live crabs are trapped in baskets, the customer is allowed a quick peep and then it's an open and shut case! The restless crabs tend to crawl away and frighten many an unsuspecting shopper.

As all fish lovers are aware, in tropical countries it is vital to eat fresh prawns or shrimps. Also the prawns and lobsters need to be de-veined carefully.

The Bengalis consider the heads of the prawns and crayfish are great delicacies. The larger ones are often fried with the hard shell intact. The *galda chingri* head when crisply fried, is a mouth-watering delicacy. The smaller heads of shrimps or prawns can jazz up even the blandest of vegetables, fries and curries.

When it comes to crabs, they must be alive and kicking. The claws and outer shell have to be prized out, the stringy strips covering the central body cleaned out. The cleaning and cutting of crabs is best left to the seller, a few extra rupees is all it takes to persuade. The eggs (coral) if any should remain, the bright orange roes are tasty. The larger crab claws should be gently hammered with a stone pestle, cracked but not broken, so that when cooked, the juices pour out, yet the white flesh remains intact. The joy of eating crabs with fingers is to pick the flesh delicately and savour the juices.

| NB. Prawns are scampi, or shrimps. |
| *Galda Chingri* is crayfish |

Tips: Sea fish can be washed with raw vinegar to keep out the 'fishy' smell.

——— RECIPES ———

Loti Chingri (taro runners with rhrimp)

Ingredients:

| Taro runner – 1 bunch |
| Shrimp – 250 gms |
| Potato – 1 (medium) |
| Mustard seed – 1 tsp |
| Poppy seed – 1 tsp |
| Sesame seed – 1 tsp |
| Turmeric powder/ paste – 1 tsp |
| Coconut (fresh) – ½ (grated) |
| Chilli powder/ paste 1 tsp |
| Mustard oil – 5 tbsp |
| Salt – to taste |

Method:

Scrape taro runners and cut into small pieces. Boil in water with salt and drain.

Cut potatoes in thin strips. Grind poppy mustard and sesame seeds to a paste. Smear shrimps with salt and turmeric, fry lightly and keep aside.

Heat oil in another pan and fry potatoes till golden. Add grated coconut, ground spices and turmeric and chilli powders. Fry, then add shrimps, salt and little water, cover. When water has come to a boil, add taro runners and cover again. Cook till dry.

Chingri Paturi (prawn in banana leaves)

Ingredients:

| Prawn – 1 kg |
| Turmeric powder/ paste – 1 tsp |
| Mustard seed – 150 gms |
| Coconut (fresh) – 1 (grated) |
| Green chilli – 4 (slit & seeded) |
| Mustard oil – 4 tbsp |
| Salt – to taste |
| Banana leaf – 6 |
| Thread to tie |

Method:

Shell and clean prawns. Grind mustard seeds, grated coconut and green chillies with salt to make a paste. Coat prawns with the paste and mustard oil, marinate for 15 minutes. Wash banana leaves. Place seasoned prawns in the centre of each banana leaf, fold and tie with thread. Fry banana leaf envelopes in a flat pan or '*tawa*' in low heat. Both sides should be fried evenly till brown. Remove thread and serve.

OPTION:

This preparation can also be cooked in microwave oven.

Chingri Shorshe Bhape (steamed prawn in mustard sauce) | Serves six

Ingredients:

Prawn – 750 gms

Mustard oil – 3 tbsp

Mustard seed – 3 tbsp

Green chilli – 3 (slit & seeded)

Coconut (fresh) – 3 ½ tbsp (grated)

Salt and sugar – to taste

Method:

Shell and clean prawns. Grind the mustard seeds, green chillies, grated coconut with a pinch of salt. Smear prawns with this paste, raw mustard oil, salt and sugar, place in a pan. Cook covered over a low flame or bake in an microwave oven. No need to add water. Simmer till prawns are tender and the gravy is thick.

Chingri Machher Malai Curry (prawn in coconut gravy) | Serves six

Ingredients:

Prawn – 6 large (600 gms)

Onion paste – 1½ tbsp

Ginger paste – 1 tbsp

Coconut (fresh) – 1 (grated)

Bay leaf – 2

Green chilli – 4 (slit & seeded)

Garam masala – Cinnamon 1″, clove 4, green cardamom 4 (whole)

Ghee – 2 tbsp or (mustard oil/ white oil may be a healthier alternative to use)

Salt & sugar – to taste

Method:

Marinate prawns with ½ tsp onion and ginger paste and a pinch of salt. Soak grated coconut in warm water for some time, squeeze to extract milk.

Heat ghee or oil in a pan, add bay leaves and whole *garam masala*.

Add rest of the paste, fry for some time, then put the marinated prawns. Fry prawns, turning over to cook evenly. Add coconut milk, sugar and salt, cook till done. Garnish with green chillies and serve hot with rice.

Tips: To keep the micro-oven odour free, keep cloves and 2/3 Disprin tablets in the corner of the oven. This helps keep out cockroaches from cupboards as well.

Galda Chingrir Matha Bhaja (fried crayfish head)

Serves six

Ingredients:

Prawn head – 12 (The outer shell and black elements must be discarded)

Rice flour * – 1 ½ cup made into thick batter

Ginger & garlic paste – 1 tbsp

Green chilli paste – 1 tsp

Mustard oil – 150 gms

Salt – to taste

* Options – use *besan* or chick pea flour

Method:

Clean prawn heads and marinate in ginger, garlic and green chilli paste for 30 minutes.

Heat oil. Dip prawn heads in batter and fry till golden and crisp. Drain. Serve hot with boiled rice.

Chingrir Tel Jhol (prawn curry)

Serves four

Ingredients:

Prawn – 600 gms (medium sized) can be cooked with or without the heads

Onion seed – ½ tsp

Turmeric powder/ paste – 1 ½ tsp

Green chilli – 6

Mustard oil – 2 tbsp

Salt – to taste

Method:

Shell and clean prawns. Mix turmeric in a bowl with two cups of water and salt. Keep aside. Smear prawns with turmeric. Heat oil in a pan, add prawns and fry till the tails turn red. Add black onion seeds and fry. Pour turmeric water and add green chillies and salt. Cook till prawns are done.

Kankrar Jhal (crab curry)

Serves six

Ingredients:

Crab – 6 (medium sized)

Onion paste – 250 gm (finely chopped)

Ginger-garlic paste – 3 tbsp

Turmeric & coriander powder/ paste – 1 tsp

Red chilli powder/ paste – 2 tsp

Mustard oil – 100 gms

Salt – to taste

Method:

Shell crabs, gently crack claws, wash with warm water and keep aside. Heat oil in pan, fry chopped onion till golden. Add the ginger-garlic paste and other spices, fry for 3-4 minutes.

Add crab, fry for another three minutes. Pour water and salt, cover. Cook till done. Serve hot.

Rashalo Dim

— epicurean eggs

Bengal's ducks thrive in village ponds and inlets. The *deshi* chicken (village poultry) find a friendly habitat in the numerous shrubs and grassy banks of water bodies. While chicken may or may not be permissible (staunch Hindus are not permitted to eat chicken). Duck eggs are enjoyed instead.

Eggs are considered a delicacy. Hot and spicy curried eggs are a traditional accompaniment to *khichuri* and is the ubiquitous stand by when unexpected guests arrive at meal times. Spiced omelettes, fried in mustard oil and other egg recipes are very much a part of Bengali cuisine.

Eggs are also part of Kolkata's street food. The anytime 'fast' food is the omelette served with buttered toasts. Cooked in front of the customer, the eggs are broken whisked with chopped onions and green chillies. While the flat metal pan on the oven smokes, on a griddle thick slices of bread are toasted with a flick of the maker's wrists, tossed up and lathered with butter. The fresh omelette is then taken off the pan, inserted between the hot grilled toasts, served in a *'shaal pata'*, (dried leaves of a large tree), and handed to the customer. Cheap and wholesome meal. Hard boiled eggs are shelled, served with ground pepper, salt and chillies.

Here are a few recipes. Picnic without boiled or curried eggs are no picnic at all. Read more about picnics in *'Choruibhati'* chapter.

Tips: To make an omelette soft, add a little lemon juice to the beaten egg.

——— RECIPES ———

Hanser Dimer Dalna (duck egg curry)

| Serves six

Ingredients:

Duck's egg – 6 (hard boiled)

Potato – 6 (300 gms)

Green chilli – 4 (slit and seeded)

Turmeric powder/ paste – 1 ½ tsp

Red chilli powder/ paste – 1 tsp

Cumin seed – 1 tsp

Cumin powder/ paste – 1 tsp

Coriander powder/ paste – 1½ tsp

Ginger paste – 1tbsp

Bay leaves – 2 pcs

Garam masala paste – 1tsp
Garam masala – 4 Green cardamom,
4 cloves, cinnamon 2" (whole)

Mustard oil – 50 gms

Ghee – 1tbsp

Salt & sugar – to taste

Method:

Wash, peel and cut potatoes into quarters. Remove shell from boiled eggs, slit each at least in three places. Rub the eggs with ½ tsp turmeric and a pinch of chilli paste and fry till reddish yellow, remove from oil and keep aside. Now fry potatoes to golden brown, drain and keep aside. Put some more oil in pan, heat, add bay leaves, cumin seed and whole *garam masala and* fry. Put turmeric, chilli, cumin, coriander and ginger pastes with sugar and a little water. Fry till spices release oil, now add fried potatoes and fry for another 5 minutes, add 2–3 cups of water (preferably warm), cover and simmer till almost done. Put fried eggs and green chillies, boil for another 5 minutes, add *garam masala* with ghee before removing from fire.

Dimer Devil (devilled egg)

Ingredients:

Egg – 8 (hard boiled)
Minced meat – 500 gms
Beaten egg – 1
Ginger/ garlic paste – 1 tbsp
Onion – 1 tbsp ((finely chopped)
Garam masala powder – 1 tsp
Gram flour (besan) – 1 tbsp
Turmeric powder/ paste – 1 tsp
Chilli powder/ paste – 1tsp
Sunflower oil – 3 tbsp
Salt – to taste

Method:

Shell boiled eggs and keep aside. In a wok, heat oil and fry onions, ginger/ garlic paste and turmeric, when slightly brown add minced meat and salt. Fry well, add a cup of water. Simmer till meat is tender. Add gram flour. Stir well, till meat is dry. Remove from heat. Cool and knead in the beaten egg and *garam masala*. Divide the cooked minced meat into 8 balls. Flatten each ball in the palm of your hand and carefully place one boiled egg in the middle. Coat each egg individually with the meat mixture, dip in the remaining beaten egg and deep fry. Serve with, lemon wedges, onion rings and green chillies.

Dim Aalur Tarkari (egg potato curry)

Ingredients:

Egg – 6 (hard boiled)
Potato – 400 gms (medium sized)
Onion – 200 gm (finely chopped)
Garlic clove – 4 (finely chopped)
Ginger paste – 1tbsp
Turmeric powder/ paste – 1 ½ tsp
Red chilli powder /paste – 1 tsp
Green chilli – 4 (slit and seeded)
Bay leaves – 2 pcs
Garam masala (whole) – 4 Green cardamom, 4 cloves, cinnamon 2 inch)
Mustard oil – 2 tbsp
Salt & sugar – to taste

Method:

Wash, boil, peel and cut potatoes into halves, and keep aside. Shell boiled eggs, slit each egg lengthwise at least in three places. Rub the eggs with ½ tsp turmeric and a pinch of chilli paste and fry till golden, remove from pan and keep aside. Add more oil and heat. Add bay leaves, and whole *garam masala*, chopped garlic, chopped onion, chilli, turmeric, ginger paste with sugarand a little water. Fry till spices release oil, now add boiled potatoes and salt, fry in low heat for 5 minutes, add 2–3 cups of water (preferably warm), cover and simmer till almost done. Add eggs and green chillies, boil till done. Serve hot.

Chutney

Chatpata Chutney
– sweet & tangy

*"All things, chickeney and mutt'ny
Taste better by far when served with chutney."*

– John F Mackay

In Bengali, the verb *'chat'* means 'to lick'. The word chutney therefore has echoes of this meaning and is considered a delectable, finger licking temptation - piquant, sweet and tangy – that rounds off a hearty meal and is considered to have digestive properties. Even when concocting the chutney, the cooks in eastern India are clever and use morsels of leftovers, fish heads and assorted sour items picked from the vegetable patch to make this finale almost irresistible. *Chutneys* or *tauk* can be made from local olives, berries, raw mangoes, plums, pineapples and other seasonal fruits or vegetables. For weddings and other feasts, the *chutney* is invariably accompanied by crisply fried *papads*.

Chutneys made with *'gur'* or molasses and sugar can be preserved. Long after the seasons for mangoes or tomatoes have passed. The chutneys add piquancy and a tangy touch to chops and cutlets.

─── RECIPES ───

Amer Chutney (mango chutney)

Ingredients:

Green mango – 4

Sugar – 4 tsp or according to taste

Cumin seed – 1 tsp (roasted and ground)

Raisin – A fistful

Panch phoron – 1 tsp

Mustard/ sunflower oil – 1 tsp

Method:

Cut peeled or unpeeled green mangoes in wedges, discard seeds. Heat oil in a pan, temper with *panch phoron* add mangoes, fry for few minutes, add water, bring to boil. Then add sugar stir frequently to get a thick consistency.

Add raisins boil for few minutes then sprinkle the ground cumin seed powder and remove from fire.

Anaraser Chutney (pineapple chutney)

Ingredients:

Pineapple – 1 (medium size)

Sugar – 500 gms (or according to taste)

Ginger – 50 gms

Lemon – 1

Vinegar – 2 tsp

Salt – ½ tsp

Method:

Peel pineapple and shred or cut into small bits. Mince ginger. Boil shredded pineapple bits in low heat, add a little water, vinegar and ginger. Add sugar and stir, till pineapple is soft. Finally add lemon juice and salt. Remove from fire. Mango chutney can be made this way.

Khejur Amshottor Chutney (date and mango preserve chutney)

Ingredients:

Tomato – 500 gms

Mango preserve (aam papad) – One (250 gms packet)

Date – 100 gms

Sunflower oil – a little

Panch phoron – ½ tsp

Sugar – 300 gms

Method:

Blanch tomatoes, slip off skin and pass through a strainer to remove seeds. Chop mango preserve into small pieces. Halve the dates and take out seeds. Heat oil in a pan, temper with *panch phoron*. Add tomato puree, dates and mango preserve. When mixture comes to a boil, stir in the sugar.

Cook till chutney is thick.

Jalpaier Chutney (olive chutney)

Serves four

Ingredients:

Olive – 200 gms (ripe and soft)

Sugar – 200gms

Raisin – 50gms

Salt – ½ tsp

Water less than a cup

Method:

Boil olives in water with a little salt. When olives start to melt add sugar and the raisins. Stir till olives are cooked. The olives may be seeded when boiled.

Tomato Chutney

Serves four

Ingredients:

Tomato – 500 gms

Ginger – 50 gms (peeled & finely chopped)

Raisins – 100 gms

Dried red chilli – 2 (whole)

Sugar – 250 gms

Vinegar – 2 tbsp

Salt – ½ tsp

Method:

Wash and cut tomatoes into quarters, boil in enough water for a chutney consistency. Add all the sugar in the same pot, add finely sliced ginger and dried red chillies, raisins, vinegar and salt. Cook till tomatoes have melted.

Kooler Chutney (Indian plum chutney)

Serves four

Ingredients:

Indian plum – 200 gms (Kool)

Mustard seed – 1tsp

Refined oil – 1 tbsp

Dried red chilli – 2 (whole)

Sugar – 200 gms

Salt – ½ tsp

Method:

Remove stalks and break plum with fingers to let out flesh. Leave seeds in. Heat oil in a pan, temper with mustard seeds and dried red chillies. Pour plum, fry for two minutes, add salt and ½ cup water. Bring to boil, add sugar, Cook till the chutney is thick.

Tips: To prepare chutney quickly, add 2 teaspoons dried mango powder, 1 teaspoon cumin powder, little chilli powder and salt to taste in a cup of water. Add sugar if you like. Boil for 5 minutes

—— RAW CHUTNEYS AND PICKLES ——

Fresh seasonal produce can make appetizing accompaniments.

Kancha Aamer Chatpat Chutney

Serves four

(uick green mango pickle)

Ingredients:	**Method:**
Raw green mango – 3 or 4 peeled and chopped finely	Mix all ingredients in a bowl, toss and serve.
Piquant green chilli – 3 or 4 chopped finely	
Mustard oil – ½ tsp	
Salt & sugar – to taste	

Batabi Lebur Salad (pummelo)

Serves four

Method:

Cut pummelo and take out the pink flesh from each segment, remove all seeds.

Mix with salt, sugar and chopped green chillies.

• Raw Guava can be also used to make a seasonal salad.

Ilish Machher Tauk or Ambal

See Machher Rani – queen of fish (*illish* chapter)

Kucho Chingrir Tauk

(Method same as illish machher tauk. Replace *illish* with shrimps)

Mishti

Mishti Mukh

— sweet truth

"Aamsotto dudhe pheli, tahate kadali dali,
sandesh makhia dia tate.
Hapus hupus sabdo, charidik nistabdho,
pipilika kandia jaye pate" *

— Rabindranath Tagore

Readers may or may not be aware that Bengal was the birthplace of the famous *rosogolla* and *sandesh*. Every road in Kolkata has a sweet shop. The shops have sign boards declaring their specialities. They may look shabby but the rows of *sandesh* (cottage cheese cakes) various balls of maroon, white and orange doused in syrups are delicious. Any and every occasion demands sweets. Sweetmeats are not just served as 'afters'. Sweets are for greeting guests, (invited or uninvited!) be it early morning or late at night. It is a polite gesture of goodwill.

Home made sweets tell another story. These delicacies are mastered by carefully watching and lots of practice. Tenderly prepared by mothers and aunts, the home made sweets are also a part of festivals and special occasions. These sweets are rarely found in sweetmeat shops. The ingredients are often seasonal, the origins hark back to village life or traditions set by country folk. We have picked a handful of easy to prepare recipes for our readers.

* "Mix mango preserves with milk, add ripe bananas and sweetmeat
Listen, then to the slurps and smacks, and all else is silent and
the poor starving ants crawl quietly away to mourn."

—— RECIPES ——

Elojhelo (crispy delights)

Serves four

Ingredients:

Flour – 200 gms

Sunflower oil – 150 gms

Sugar – 300 gms

Salt – ½ tsp

Method:

Make a thick syrup with sugar and water. Sieve together flour and salt. Rub in 75 gms oil, add water to make a firm dough. Make flat round cakes from the dough and roll each out in a circle. With a sharp knife, make six long, vertical slits in each circle, taking care to leave the ends intact. Holding the top and bottom ends, roll the cut circles and press each end with finger and thumb to seal. Deep fry till golden and crisp. Drop them in syrup and take them out when well soaked.

Gaja (floury crisps)

Serves four

Ingredients:

Flour – 200 gms

Sunflower oil – 150 gms

Sugar – 300 gms

Salt – a pinch

Method:

Make a thick syrup with sugar and water. Sieve together flour and salt. Rub in 75 gms of oil and make a firm dough, add water if needed. Roll into a large and thin square piece of dough, then cut rolled out dough into diamond shaped 1" pieces. Deep fry these golden brown. Drop the *gajas* in syrup for a few minutes before serving.

Narkel Naru (coconut balls)

Serves four

Ingredients:

Coconut (Fresh) – 1 (medium)

Sugar/ molasses – 125 gms

Cardamom powder – 2 pinches

Ghee or white oil – 100 gms

Method:

Scrape off the coconut flesh and mix with sugar or molasses. Stir over heat. Cook till the mixture comes off the sides of the pan. Mix in the cardamom powder. Cool slightly and roll the mix into round shaped balls.

Chandrapuli (coconut cakes)

Serves four

Ingredients:

Dried thickened milk (*kheer*) – 100gms

Cardamom powder – 2 pinches

Coconut (Fresh) – 1

Sugar – 200 gms

Method:

Scrape out coconut flesh and grind to a paste. Mix this well with the sugar and dried thickened milk. Heat and stir. Cook till the mixture comes off the sides of pan. Add cardamom powder. Cool slightly and press them into moulds available in Kolkata markets. Or shape them in decorative designs.

Traditional Malpoaa (sweet fritters)

Serves four

Ingredients:

Flour – 200 gms

Milk – ½ litre

Dried thickened milk (*Kheer*) – 200 gms

Semolina – 50 gms

Sugar – 600 gms

Raisins – 2 tbsp

Fennel/ aniseed seed – 1 tbsp

Ghee or oil – for frying

Method:

Mix sugar with two cups of water, boil to make a thick syrup and keep aside. Combine flour with milk and a cup of water to make a smooth batter. Add semolina and '*kheer*' to this mix. The batter should be medium thick and not watery. Add raisins and fennel seeds. Drop dollops of the batter into hot oil and fry till light brown, patting down to get individual circular shapes. Soak in the syrup for two to three hours. Then remove from syrup and place in a platter.

Simply Delicious Ma's Malpoaa

The method is the same as above but without the raisins and fennel seeds. Just make a batter with thickened milk and flour. Do not add water. Mix well. Take a ladle or a deep round spoon to spoon out the batter into steaming hot white oil. Fry the pan cakes well one at a time, turning them carefully. When the pan cakes turn maroon, remove from fire. Drain excess oil and drop them into syrup. The syrup is made by boiling sugar in a pot of water. The syrup should be sticky but not watery.

Take them out individually and serve.

Ranga Alur Puli (sweet potato dumplings)

Serves four

Ingredients:

Sweet potato – 500 gms
(boiled, peeled and mashed)

Sugar – 700 gms

Dried thickened milk (*kheer/khoya*) – 50gms

Flour – 2 tbsp

Sunflower oil mixed with ghee – for
deep frying

Method:

Make a syrup with 600 gms sugar and
three cups of water. Keep aside.

Mix together thickened milk, sweet
potato mash, and flour to bind. Next
form oblong shapes, with tapered ends.
Fry in hot oil with a little ghee, when the
patties are brown, soak them in syrup.

Patishapta (bengali pan cake)

Serves four

Ingredients:

Flour – 200 gms

Semolina – 100 gms

Dried thickened milk (*kheer/khoya*) – 200 gms

Cardamom powder – 4

Milk – 1 cup

Sugar – 250 gms

Sunflower oil – 100 gms

Alternative fillings: Freshly scraped
coconut and winter molasses or *notun
gur* make wonderful fillings.

Method:

Make a thick batter with flour, semolina,
milk, a little sugar. Keep aside for at least
an hour.

Mix 200 gms sugar with dried thickened
milk and fry in 1½ tbsp oil. Add
cardamom powder, keep aside. Place
a griddle on fire, oil it thoroughly, pour
two tbsp batter on the centre of the
griddle, spread it evenly in a circular
shape with a spoon. Fry in low heat till
it comes off the griddle, add the 2 tsp
fillings in the centre of each pan cake.
Now roll pan cake and seal. Remove
from fire.

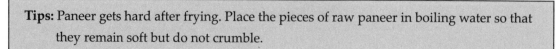

Tips: Paneer gets hard after frying. Place the pieces of raw paneer in boiling water so that
they remain soft but do not crumble.

Kheer Kamla (condensed milk pudding with presh orange)

Ingredients:

Milk – 1 litre

Sugar – 75 gms

Orange – 4 (fresh and ripe)

Method:

Peel oranges, take out segments. Open segments take out orange pulp, carerfully discard the pips and keep aside. Boil milk with sugar stir constantly till thick and of 'saucy' consistency. One litre milk should reduce to ½ litre. Let the milk cool. Add the orange pulp, stir and refrigerate. Serve chilled.

Condensed milk can be mixed with a cup of boiling milk and stirred to get the right *'payesh'* consistency.

Payesh (rice pudding)

Ingredients:

Milk – 2 litres (full cream)

Basmati/Gobindobhog rice – 1 cup (200 gms)

Sugar – according to taste

Bay leaf – 2

Green cardamom – 4

Raisin – 25 gms

A few chopped pistachios to garnish

Method:

Boil milk with green cardamom and bay leaves for 20 minutes. Add rice and stir frequently, cook till rice is half done, add sugar and the raisins. Cook till rice is soft. Remove from fire. Garnish with chopped pistachios.

Nolen Gurer Payesh (rice pudding with special molasses)

Ingredients:

Milk – 2 litres (full cream)

Basmati/Gobindobhog rice – 1 cup (200 gms)

Date palm molasses (*notun gur*) – 150 gms

Raisins – 25 gms

Method:

The method is the same as for *'Payesh'*, only add date palm molasses instead of sugar, the former being a very special kind of molasses available only in winter. It has a delicate fragrance and is used to enrich sweet seasonal delicacies.

Chhanar Payesh (cottage cheese pudding)

Cottage cheese is not paneer. Cottage cheese (*Chhana*) is made from fresh milk which has curdled with the help of lime juice or acids and strained to give it a thick consistency.)

Ingredients:

Cottage cheese – 100 gms

Milk – 1 litre (full cream)

Sugar – 150 gms

Raisin – 25 gms

Pistachio nut – 2 tbsp (finely chopped)

Rose water – 2 tsp

Rose petals to garnish

Method:

Tie cottage cheese in a piece of cloth and hang for some time to drain out water completely. Boil milk with sugar stir constantly till it becomes thick. Add cottage cheese and raisins, stir for few minutes. Remove from fire, cool, add rose water. Sprinkle chopped pistachios and garnish with rose petals.

Didi's Bhapa Doi (baked yoghurt)

Ingredients:

Sweet condensed milk – 1 can (300 ml)

Fresh, whole milk to dilute condensed milk – 1 cup

Sweet yoghurt – 250 gms

Raisin – 25gm.

Finely chopped pistachio nuts to garnish – 25 gms

Method:

Pre-heat oven to 350⁰F. Mix together condensed milk and fresh milk. Boil milk mixture in a saucepan, stirring constantly. Do not allow to curdle or stick to the bottom of the pan. When mixture reaches a smooth consistency (after about 15 minutes), remove from stove and let it cool. Cover saucepan to prevent skin forming on the surface of the mixture. Beat the yoghurt in a bowl till smooth, without letting it become watery. When milk mixture has cooled, whisk in the yoghurt slowly till it is smooth, without any lumps. No need to add sugar as condensed milk is sweetened. Pour mixture into a square, shallow, rectangular oven proof glass dish. Cover tightly with foil. Place the ovenproof dish in a large metal container filled with with hot water. Steam the pudding in the oven or microwave for about 30 mins. Remove from oven and fold back the foil partly. Test the surface of the *doi* with a finger tip. It should be firm to the touch. If not, return to the oven and bake for another 10/15 mins.

Cool in fridge and then decorate with raisins and dust with pistachio nuts. If desired, cut the pudding into diamond or squares before serving. Do not take the pieces out until ready to serve.

Ras Bora (lentil dumplings in syrup)

Serves four

Ingredients:

Split black lentil – 250 gms

Sugar – 500 gms

Cardamom powder – 1 tsp (optional)

Sunflower oil – 250 gms

Method:

Make syrup with 500 gms sugar and three cups of water. Keep aside.

Soak lentils overnight in water. Grind soaked lentils to make a thick paste, add cardamom powder and keep it for sometime to allow it to ferment. Heat oil in pan, make small sized balls from the paste and deep fry till golden brown, then drop them in syrup and soak them before serving.

Chhanar Murki (cottage cheese bits)

Serves four

Ingredients:

Cottage Cheese – 500 gms

Sugar – 750 gms

Cardamom powder – 1 tsp (optional)

Method:

Hang cottage cheese in a cotton sack/pouch to drain out water. Take a shallow plate or a platter with a 2" rim. Pour drained cottage cheese in it, press down with fingers so that cottage cheese sets in, should be about 1" high. Cut cottage cheese carefully into cubes. Heat 4 cups of water in a pan, pour sugar and make syrup. Now drop cottage cheese cubes in the syrup, boil continuously till dry. Sprinkle cardamom powder and remove from fire. And serve.

Tips:

- Place a piece of jaggery (*gur*) in the bottle of ghee to keep ghee fresh for longer.

- Place a small green chilli in the bowl while making curd at home. Curd will set and not become watery.

- Hang curd in a cloth if it turns sour. Curd will turn fresh when water is drained.

Jal Khabar

Jal Khabar

– high tea

*"A joy worth repeating
again and again, warm conversation,
tea, food and a friend"*

A day in the life of a Bengali is not divided by hours, but by meals. Apart from lunch and dinner, dusk is the time for *'jal khabar'*. The words literally mean liquid refreshments. More solid than liquid, to be honest, and washed down with steaming cups of tea. No Bengali can resist a snack in between meals. The heavy snacks were devised for hungry children coming home from school and office goers returning after a long day's toil. The tidbits served around 5pm-6pm set the pace for a late dinner. The tea time snacks are eaten on their own, without any cereals. However *luchis* (fluffy bread made from flour) is considered very much a part of *jal khabar*. Home made sweets are prepared with care and served to special guests for *'jal khabar'*.

——— RECIPES ———

Luchi (fFried flour bread)

Ingredients:

Flour – 500 gms

Sunflower oil – 300 gms

Salt – ½ tsp

Method:

Pour flour in a bowl, add ½ tsp salt and 1 tbsp oil, mix well. Add water and make a soft dough. Now make 40 balls out of the dough. Roll into flat small circles. Carefully place rolled roundels or *luchies* in a flat tray. Heat oil in a deep pan. When oil is smoking put in rolled *luchis* one at a time, fry lightly till the *luchi* puffs up and become golden, drain and place in a platter. Fry the rest in the same way. *Luchis* should be eaten immediately, *aalur dom* is a delicious accompaniment.

Aalur Dom (potato curry)

Ingredients:

Potato – 500 gms (small sized)

Turmeric powder/ paste – 1 tsp

Red chilli powder/ paste – 1 tsp, 2 (whole)

Cumin powder/ paste – 2 tsp

Coriander powder/ paste – 1 ½ tsp

Cumin seed – 1 tsp (whole)

Ginger paste – 2 tsp

Bay leaf – 2

Lemon juice – 1 tbsp (optional)

Coriander leaf – 1 bunch (chopped)

Mustard oil – 2 tbsp

Salt & sugar – to taste

Method:

Boil potatoes, drain and remove skin. Heat oil in a pan, add whole cumin, bay leaves and fry for a minute. Add all the spice pastes with sugar and fry well. Add boiled potatoes and salt, sprinkle water, fry for another two minutes. Stir in the lemon juice and remove from fire. Garnish with chopped coriander leaves.

OPTION I:

This dish can be cooked with onion and garlic pastes as well. Use whole green cardamoms, cloves and cinnamon instead of whole cumin.

OPTION II: Add asafoetida for tempering.

Mohon Bhog (semolina pudding)

Ingredients:

Semolina (suji) – 200 gms
Milk – 1 ½ cup
Sugar – 100 gms
Sunflower oil – 2 tbsp
Ghee – 1tbsp
Raisin – 25 gms
Cashew nut – 25 gms (dry roasted)
Bay leaf – 2
Green cardamom – 4

Method:

Soak raisins in a bowl. Heat sunflower oil and ghee in a pan, add bay leaves fry, add semolina, fry till brown, then add milk, sugar and cardamom. Stir well. When semolina is cooked. Sprinkle raisins and cashew nuts.

OPTION:

Instead of milk add water.

Ghugni (yellow pea curry)

Ghugni is a curry made with soaked chick peas or whole grams. Substantial, nutritious and tasty, it can be served with a dash of lime juice, chopped chillies and onions.

Ingredients:

Yellow pea – 250 gms
Coconut (fresh) – ½ (finely chopped)
Turmeric powder/ paste – 1 tsp
Cumin powder/ paste – 1 ½ tsp
Coriander powder/ paste – 1 ½ tsp
Red chilli powder/ paste – 2 (whole)
Ginger paste – 2 tsp
Green chilli – 4 (slit and seeded)
Cumin – 1 tsp (whole)
Dried red chilli – 2 (whole)
Coriander leaf (fresh) – a bunch (chopped)
Bay leaf – 2
Tamarind juice – 1 ½ tbsp
Mustard oil – 3 tbsp
Salt & sugar – to taste

Method:

Soak yellow peas overnight. Boil with a pinch of turmeric and salt. Fry chopped coconut till golden, drain and keep aside. Heat oil in a pan, add whole cumin, red chilli and bay leaves and fry. Add rest of the spices, sugar and salt, fry till golden. Add boiled yellow peas and water simmer for 5 minutes. Add green chillies, fried coconut and stir well. Finally, add tamarind juice and remove from fire. Sprinkle chopped fresh coriander leaves before serving.

OPTION:

Onion and garlic paste can also be added, to give *ghugni* an extra zing.

Nimki (savoury bits)

Ingredients:

Flour – 500 gms

Sunflower oil – 100 gms

Onion seed – 1 tsp

Salt – ½ tsp

Method:

Pour flour in a bowl, add ½ tsp salt and one tbsp oil, then onion seed. Add water to make a firm dough and divide into large balls. Roll out each ball into flat big circles. With a sharp knife cut from top to bottom vertically and then diagonally to get small diamond shaped pieces. Place these bits on a sheet of paper and dust with flour. Deep fry the bits or *nimkis* in hot oil till golden.

◆◆

Parota (fried flatbread)

| Serves Six

Ingredients:

Flour – 500 gms

Ghee – 2 tbsp

Sunflower oil – 300 gms

Salt & sugar – to taste

Method:

Put flour in a bowl, add salt, sugar and ghee, mix well. Make a dough with water, cover with a moistened cloth and keep aside for ½ hour. Now make 15-16 balls and roll them into circles or triangles. Fry both side of *parotas* on a frying pan till golden brown. Serve with stir fired vegetables, *aalur dom* or dry and spicy meat curry (*kasha mangsho*).

◆◆

Aalur Saada Torkari (simple non- spicy potato stew)

| Serves four

Ingredients:

Potato – 500 gms (small sized)

Green chilli – 4 (slit and seeded)

Onion seed – 1 tsp

Sunflower oil – 2 tbsp

Salt & sugar – to taste

Method:

Wash and cut potatoes into cubes. Heat oil in a pan, add onion seeds and two green chillies and fry. Add potatoes, fry on low heat for 5 minutes. Add sugar, salt, green chillies and water, simmer till done. Serve hot with *luchis* or *parotas*

Matarshutir Kochuri (green pea patty)

Ingredients:

Flour – 500 gms

Green pea (without pod) – 250 gms

Asafoetida – ½ tsp

Cumin powder/ paste – 1½ tsp

Ginger paste – 1tbsp

Sunflower oil – 300 gms

Salt & sugar – to taste

Method:

Shell green peas and grind to a paste. Heat oil in a pan, add asafoetida, green pea paste, sugar, salt, cumin and ginger pastes. Fry for a few minutes and keep aside. Pour flour in a bowl, add ½ tsp salt and 1 tbsp oil. Add water and make a dough. Make 20 balls and shape each ball into a cup and fill it with mixture. Again roll into a ball, then roll out into flat circles. Heat oil in a deep pan, and deep fry the rolled *kochuris* (two to three at a time), till golden, drain and remove from fire.

Machher Kochuri (fish patty)

Ingredients:

Rui/ katla Fish * – 500 gms (pieces)

Turmeric powder/ paste – 1 tsp

Red chilli powder/ paste – 1 tsp

Garam masala powder/ paste – 1 tsp

Onion paste – 1 ½ tsp

Ginger paste – 1 tbsp

Garlic paste – 1 tsp

Flour – 500 gms

Sunflower oil – 300 gms

Salt & sugar – to taste

*Any flaky fish can be used.

Method:

Boil fish pieces with salt and turmeric. Drain, de-bone and mash fish. Heat 2 tbsp oil in a pan, add onion, ginger and garlic pastes and fry. Add mashed fish, chilli, 1 tsp sugar and salt, fry for 3–4 minutes, add *garam masala* and stir fry till mixture is dry. Remove from fire and keep aside.

Pour flour in a bowl, add 1 tsp salt and 1tbsp oil, mix it well. Pour water and make a dough. Make 20 balls and roll them into flat thin circles. Put fish filling in the centre of the rolled circle, then cover each with another circle. Brush water at the edges, and twist to seal. Heat oil in a pan. Deep fry stuffed *kochuris,* till golden. Drain before removing from fire.

Phulkopir Shingara (cauliflower-vegetable patties)

Serves eight

Ingredients:

Cauliflower – 1 (medium)

Potato – 200 gms

Green pea – 100 gms

Cumin seed – 1 tsp

Coriander seed – 1 tsp

Dried red chilli – 2 (whole)

Cumin powder/ paste – ½ tsp

Coriander powder/ paste – ½ tsp

Red chilli powder/ paste – ½ tsp

Ginger paste – 1 tsp

Clove – 4

Green cardamom – 4

Cinnamon – 1 (1")

Flour – 300 gms

Sunflower oil – 250 gms

Salt & sugar – to taste

Method:

Wash and cut cauliflower into small florets. Peel and cut potatoes into small cubes.

Roast cumin, coriander seeds and all whole spices and grind to a powder.

Heat 3 tbsp oil in a pan, fry cauliflower to golden, strain and keep aside. In the same oil put potatoes and fry for 3 minutes add fried cauliflower, green peas and all spice pastes/ powder with sugar and salt. Sprinkle some water, cover and cook till tender and dry. Remove from fire, sprinkle with ground spice powder.

Pour flour in a bowl, add ½ tsp salt and 1 tbsp oil. Add water and make a dough. Now make 15 balls and roll them into flat thin circles. Cut each one in to half and fold them to form a hollow conical shape. Fill the hollow with the vegetable filling. Press in to triangular shapes. Seal the ends, brush with water and twist the edges to seal.

Heat rest of the oil in a pan. Put in 4-5 *shingaras* at a time, deep fry till golden brown, remove from fire and drain .

OPTIONS:

Mince meat or fish make tasty fillings. Just add chopped onions, ginger and *garam masala* to the mix.

Tips:
To make crispy luchis add 1 teaspoon of suji to every 100gm of flour while making a dough.

Machher Chop (fish croquets)

Carp or any other flaky fish can be use.

Ingredients:

Rui/ katla Fish – 500 gms (cut into pieces)
Turmeric powder/ paste – 1 tsp
Red chilli powder/ paste – 1 tsp
Garam masala powder/ paste – 1 tsp
Onion paste – 1 ½ tsp
Bread crumb – 200 gms
Mustard oil – 300 gms
Ginger paste – 1 tbsp
Garlic paste – 1 tsp
Potato – 500 gms
Egg – 3 (beaten)
Salt & sugar – to taste

Method:

Boil fish with salt and turmeric. Drain, de-bone and mash. Heat two tbsp oil, add onion, ginger and garlic paste fry till light brown, then add mashed fish, chilli, 1 tsp sugar and salt, sprinkle a little water, fry for 3–4 minutes, then add *garam masala*, fry till the mixture is dry. Remove from fire and keep aside. Beat eggs in a bowl with a little salt and keep aside.

Boil potatoes, peel and mash well. Divide mashed potatoes into eight portions. Shape each portion into a cup and fill with fish mixture, Seal the filling inside and roll into an oval shape. Dip each chop into beaten egg and coat with bread crumbs. Heat oil in a pan, fry three or four chops at a time, till golden, drain and remove from the pan.

———◆◆———

Aalu Morich (peppery potatoes)

Ingredients:

Potato – 500 gms (big sized)
Pepper – 1 tbsp (freshly ground)
Sunflower oil – 2 tbsp
Onion – 2 tsp (finely chopped)
Ginger – 1 tsp (finely chopped)
Butter/ ghee for garnishing
Salt – to taste

Method:

Boil potatoes, peel and cut into cubes. Heat oil, add potatoes and stir fry. When potato edges are slightly brown, sprinkle ground papper and salt. Garnish with ghee or butter and serve.

Cha

Cha-er-biroti

– tea break

*"Come, oh come, ye tea-thirsty
restless ones – the kettle boils,
bubbles and sings, musically."*

— Rabindranath Tagore

It is not surprising that Bengalis love tea. The east is a tea growing country. Assam and the Dooars are situated in the undulating lush plains, where the mighty river Brahmaputra and its tributaries flow, making the regions perfect for growing strong, rich teas. However it is the Darjeeling variety that is most prized by connoisseurs.

Darjeeling lies in the northern fringes of Bengal, in the shadows of the splendid Himalayas. At a height of nearly 7000 ft above sea level. The emerald valleys are crested by the majestic Kanchenjungha icy peaks. And it is a treasure trove of the world's finest teas – the bespoke variety is labeled the champagne of teas. Very expensive and very special, these teas can only grow in the districts of Darjeeling. The climate, the soil and the high altitude make Darjeeling teas the world's finest. Redolent with exquisite flavour and imbued with a delicate fragrance, this special tea is the choice of Emperors of Japan and select few in Germany and Europe. And greatly appreciated by tea connoisseurs, here.

A word of praise, about the strong CTC Assam and Dooars teas must be said as well. This rich brew stirred with plenty of milk and sugar is wonderfully refreshing. The roadside cafes, serve strong, sweet tea which is usually made with Assam CTC or dust teas.

The health giving properties of tea are now universally known. Tea is rich in antioxidants and a healthy alternative to aerated cold drinks. No wonder it is said that tea is the best drink of the day.

When *Harir Khobor* magazine was published, a chapter was devoted to tea in every issue. Readers wrote about their own experiences and 'tea break' moments. Fragments from the collection are brought to you here.

──────── NEW TWIST TO AN OLD BREW ────────

It's a monsoon afternoon, I hear a voice call out, "How are you, Didi? (Elder sister)". I see Brindaban smiling, kettle in hand. With a broad grin, Brindaban takes out a white, plastic tumbler, pours golden liquid into it, then mixes sugar, lemon juice and a pinch of rock salt. A few sips of the brew, thirst quenched. I comment, "I haven't tried this before."

"Yes, Didi," Brindaban says modestly. "Nowadays I make lemon tea, sometimes with chatpata masala (spices). That will be one rupee seventy-five paise." Placing the money in Brindaban's outstretched hand, I smile. His brew is new but he is the same old calculating businessman! He counts his day's earnings very carefully outside the Telegraph office. Eminent writers, journalists or film directors, none escape Brindaban's tea or hawk-eyed scrutiny. It is not unusual for a customer to ask for a cup and declare, "no change, will pay tomorrow!" Brindaban sells tea and at intervals jots down, his earnings and dues. One day I had a cup of his lemony brew but was in a rush to get into a taxi, Brindaban said... 'Don't worry pay me tomorrow, here have a cup". I rushed off with cup in hand. Next day, there was no Brindaban. I searched. He was not in his usual place. Days passed, I got a new job. The dues were never paid, he left me with twinge of guilt, and a keepsake. The recipe for a delicious lemony hot tea. I'm in his debt forever.

──────── TEA IN A COLD CLIMATE? ────────

I remember another time and another place, when a cup of tea, saved my soul. Up in the mountains at an altitude of nearly 10,000 ft, we had gone trekking. Dark clouds loomed... as we climbed up towards the monastery up on the hill. When a sudden downpour exploded blurring the mountains and scenery. The landscape turned into a shimmering canvas of water colours. I shivered helplessly as bone chilling, icy winds and rain lashed against me. There was no escape, no shelter, no respite. I almost fainted with cold. The temperature must have been below zero. Far ahead, on the slopes, we spotted a small shabby hut.

It was a shelter, we had to get there. Slowly we inched towards it. Huddled in my thin raincoat, breathing hard with exertion and shivering with cold I resolutely trudged up. Every step was agonizing. Till I reached the hut and entered – shelter at last! Rescue was at hand! It was a teashop! Tea was on the boil in an enormous cauldron over a wood fire. All of us warmed our hands and feet by the open fire.

The distant mountain peaks, the moving stream of people and the dense pine forests looked surrealistic. I was in a distant world.

My thoughts were broken, as the kind old man the tea shop owner, held out a bowl of streaming hot tea and affectionately asked me if I were lost. I was lost in a strange cold world. His kind words and hot tea brought me back to life. A warm feeling of comfort came over me. One sip of that hot sweet brew – and I felt that all was right with the world.

———— TRAVELLERS' TEA ————

There's a certain magic and satisfaction of having tea at railway stations.

Often, while travelling in a train, one wakes up in the middle of the night with a jolt. The rhythmic movement of wheels comes to a sudden stop, it could be at some obscure dimly-lit station. The name on the board is insignificant, the shadowy figures indistinct, but the chaiwalla's cry of 'garam chai' is comforting if not reassuring. It is not a ghost town after all! A tea vendor appears out of the darkness, a kettle and earthen bowl in hand. 'Chai garam!', he calls out and drowsily a fellow passenger stretches out his arm for a bowl of hot tea. The steaming liquid is poured carefully into the earthenware, money extracted and handed out, change given back in coins and the man turns to the next customer. What's the time? It hardly matters. It could be midnight or 3 am. The smell of

the terracotta bowl combined with the flavour of tea make the humdrum brew taste ambrosial. Tea soothes and satisfies. The tired traveller jump starts again. The train begins to move, the slushy, hot tea is held gingerly with two fingers, careful not spill a drop.

Tea breaks at various stations are always welcome. Tea relieves boredom. Tea, the best alternative to water. Most favoured, when sipped in terracotta bowls. (the anticipation of smashing them adds to the flavour). The journey continues and another sleepy station approaches. Now it's sunset. Birds fly home. In the grey half shadows of light and darkness, one listens, there it is the comforting cry of 'chai'. Night is falling, the chaiwalla disappears slowly from view as the rain chugs along. Tomorrow is another day. For travellers and tea.

———— DARJEELING TEA ————

Darjeeling tea has no equal. So rare and unique is its flavour that it cannot be replicated. The very special attributes of Darjeeling tea are its incomparable flavour, exotic fragrance and amber colour. A result of nature's unique blend of ingredients.

A perfect cup

Take fresh water from the cold tap and boil. Rinse the teapot with hot water. Put one tea spoonful of Darjeeling tea for each cup in to the pot (for a rich cup an extra spoon of tea may be added). Pour boiling water in to the pot. Cover and brew for three minutes. Strain tea into cups. Add milk and sugar to taste.

Iced Tea

Take fresh water from the cold tap and boil. Put one tea spoonful of Darjeeling tea in to tea pot for each cup in to the pot. Pour boiling water in to the pot. Cover and brew for three minutes. Fill three fourth of a large glass tumbler with ice cubes. Pour tea from the pot. Add sugar and sliced lemon to taste. Cool for few minutes and serve.

Lemon Tea

Take fresh water from the cold tap and boil. Put one tea spoonful of Darjeeling tea in to tea pot for each cup in to the pot. Pour boiling water in to the pot. Cover and brew for three minutes. Pour tea in cups, add few drops of lemon juice and sugar to taste. You can add a pinch of rock salt. Serve hot.

Ginger Tea

Take three cups of water and one cup of milk in a sauce pan, bring to boil. Add three tea spoonful of CTC leaf/ dust tea and sugar to taste, boil for a minute, then add grated ginger, boil for another minute. Remove from fire. Strain, pour in to cups and serve hot.

For spiced tea add cardamom and clove instead of ginger.

Thakumar jhuli

Thakumar Jhuli
– grandmothers' specials

"Grandmothers are a delightful blend of laughter, caring deeds, wonderful stories, delicious recipes – all served with love"

– Anonymous

Not every Bengali will have a skeleton in the cupboard, but most Bengali families will have a secret recipe that has been guarded and handed down generation after generation. The origin of the authentic Bengali recipe may have begun when the mother-in-law took charge of her little daughter-in-law, (in the early 19th century or 20th century, the bride may have come into the family as a mere child of 9 or 10). She would have to follow her mother-in-law's instructions. She would be taught a great deal of do's and don'ts, rights and wrongs and rites and rituals. The young bride would learn the family's specialities as well as the taboos. The newly wed would also bring some of her own recipes from home. learnt from her mother. Not just to share but to show off her cooking skills.

In the olden days, the bride-to-be in her first encounter with the in-laws would be asked a set of questions on the art of cooking. Does the child know which *'phoron'* or tempering goes with which *daal*? Does she know how to cook hilsa fish? Does she know how the potatoes are cut for a *chorchori*? Is garlic permitted in fish *jhol*? So on and so forth. Having passed this test, the girl would then be judged by her demeanor, modesty, skin and hair!

My husband's grandmother "Shailabala Devi", a *probashi* (immigrant) Bangali, travelled far from home, in the 1900's (yet again from Jessore), and set up house with her husband, Dr. J. K. Sen in old Delhi. She soon became a competent housewife and cook, who could feed a large number of people with vegetables from her own kitchen garden and limited resources.

Meals were served to many devotees of Sri Anandamoyee Ma, (a saint) who came to stay with her large entourage in Hanuman Road. Shailabala Devi sold her recepies to newspapers to support Mahatma Gandhi's independence movement.

It is interesting to note, that brides of Bengal brought with them recipes from their own states or districts. Each district in Bengal has a particular delicacy. Burdwan is famous for its *kalai daal* and *posto charchchari*. East Bengal is known for their variety of fish delicacies and liberal use of chilllies. Faridpur, Dhaka or Chittagong had their own 'hot' flavours, while the West Bengalis are known to add a pinch of sugar to even savoury dishes.

While producing *"Harir Khobor"*, we requested many seniors to contribute their favourite recipes. The response was overwhelming, many including a grandfather, willingly sent us recipes which we consider cherished gifts. The recipes were learnt long ago and remembered fondly to be passed on to the next generation. Here is a classic collection.

Tips:

- Sprinkle salt on dusters or cloth before wiping the dining table, this keeps flies away.

- Smear soap under cooking utensils to prevent black stains.

- Fry sliced onions with a little sugar, to make onions golden brown.

- Lightly brown suji (semolina) in a pan (without oil) and store for future use.

——— RECIPES ———

Rajshahi Chapor Ghonto (vegetables with split pea cakes) | Serves four

Ingredients:

Split pea lentils (*mator daal*) – 200 gms

Potato – 200 gms

Cauliflower – ½ (make florets)

Cabbage – 250 gms

Green pea – 150 gms (without pods)

Mustard seed – 1 tsp

Bay leaf – 2

Ginger paste – 2 tbsp

Coconut (fresh) – ½ cup (grated)

Garam masala powder/ paste – ½ tsp

Green chilli – 6 (slit and seeded)

Mustard oil – 100 gms

Ghee – 1 tbsp

Salt & sugar – to taste

Method:

Soak split peas overnight. Wash, peel and cut potatoes into small cubes. Chop cabbage finely.

Drain split peas, grind coarsely with two green chillies and a pinch of salt. Make small round shaped balls and fry in mustard oil till crisp and brown. Now fry potatoes and cauliflowers separately and keep aside. Heat more oil in the same pan, temper with mustard seeds, bay leaves and two green chillies. Add chopped cabbage, ginger paste and green peas, fry for few minutes, add fried potatoes, cauliflowers, salt, sugar and a little water, cover and simmer till vegetables are tender, add grated coconut, green chillies and fried lentil balls. Add ghee and *garam masala*. Stir well and remove from fire.

——— ॐ ———

Badamer Borfi (nut squares) | Serves four

Ingredients:

Peanut – 250 gms

Cashew nut – 50 gms

Thickened or condensed milk – 50 gms

Sugar – 300 gms

Water – 300 ml

Method:

Roast nuts, grind to powder and keep aside. Boil water, add sugar make a thick syrup, add powdered nuts, stir well for a few minutes then add thickened or condensed milk, stir to make a thick paste. Remove from fire. Place on a deep plate, spread evenly, when cool and well set, cut into squares.

Lau Diye Bhaja Mooger Daal
(roasted split green gram with bottle gourd)

| Serves four

Ingredients:

Split green gram (*moog daal*) – 250 gms

Bottle gourd – 500 gms

Turmeric powder/ paste – 1 tsp

Green chilli – 4 (slit and seeded)

Sunflower oil – 1 tbsp

Bay leaf – 2

Dried red chilli – 2 (whole)

Fenugreek seed – ½ tsp

Coriander leaf – a small bunch

Salt & Sugar – to taste

Method:

Fry lentils without oil, till they are golden. Cut gourd into cubes. Boil lentils, add turmeric paste and salt. When lentils and vegetable are done, add green chillies.

In another pan, heat oil add bay leaves, red chillies and fenugreek seeds, fry, pour over the lentils. Add sugar to taste.

Garnish with chopped coriander leaves.

Mulor Tauk (sweet and sour horse radish)

| Serves four

Ingredients:

Horse radish – 250 gms

Tamarind pulp – 4 tbsp

Date molasses – 150 gms

Coconut (fresh) – 1 cup (grated)

Mustard seed – 1 tsp

Turmeric powder/ paste – 1 tsp

Refined oil – 1 ½ tbsp

Salt – to taste

Method:

Wash and dice radish in thin round slices. Mix tamarind pulp in ½ cup of water to make a sauce. Heat oil in a pan temper with mustard seeds, add radish fry till light brown. Pour a cup of water, add salt, turmeric paste. Simmer till tender. Now add grated coconut, tamarind sauce and molasses. Simmer to thick consistency. Remove from fire.

Tips:
- Place a pinch of soda bicarbonate in an open container inside the refrigerator to keep away bad odour.

- To clean the freezer, rub a little glycerine on the sides, ice will come off quickly.

Amidst all kinds of memorabilia I found the following recipes that an anxious mother sent to a daughter abroad, who hardly ever entered a kitchen. From those scraps I salvaged easy-to- make and simple recipes. These recipes may be useful for young people trying their hand at cooking.

Begunpora (roasted brinjal)

Serves six

Ingredients:

Brinjal – 2 (large)

Mustard oil – 2 tsp

Onion – 1 large (chopped)

Chilli – 2/3 (chopped)

Tomato – 2 (optional)

Coriander leaf – 1 tsp (chopped)

Lemon juice – 2 tsp

Salt – to taste

Method:

Roast whole brinjals (do not take out the stem) over a grill or flame, till skin becomes charred. Remove skin. The process is easy, use a polythene bag, place the roasted brinjal inside the bag and rub, holding the stem, the skin will come off. When the brinjals have been skinned, discard the stem, mash brinjal with onions, tomatoes, green chillies, mustard oil, salt and coriander leaves. Add a squeeze of lemon juice. Good with hot chapattis.

Another Method:

Heat oil in a wok, break two eggs into it and stir with the mashed brinjals and all other ingredients.

———— 𝒢 ————

Bandhakopir Sada Torkari (simple cabbage fry)

Serves six

Ingredients:

Cabbage – 750 gms

Mustard oil – 2 tbsp

Onion seed – ½ tsp

Green chilli – 5 (slit and seeded)

Salt & sugar – to taste

Method:

Wash and chop cabbage finely. Heat oil, add onion seeds and 2 green chillies and fry. Add cabbage and fry for two minutes, add rest of the green chillies, salt and sugar, cover the pan and cook till done. Garnish with fresh coriander.

Piaj Tomato Diye Daal (lentils with onion and tomatoes)

Serves four

Ingredients:

Red lentil (*mushur daal*) – 200 gms

Onion – 3

Tomato – 4

Mustard oil – 2 tsp

Green chilli – 5 (slit and seeded)

Turmeric powder/ paste – 1 tsp

Lots of fresh coriander to garnish

Salt – to taste

Method:

Wash lentils and keep aside. Cut onions and tomatoes into quarters. Heat oil in pan add onions and 2 green chillies, fry till onions are soft. Add lentils, tomatoes, turmeric and green chillies, fry for 2 minutes. Add three cups of water and salt, cook till done. Garnish with fresh coriander.

Another delicious Method: add roasted garlic to the broth.

⎯⎯⎯⎯ ༄ ⎯⎯⎯⎯

Sheem Charchchari (stir-fried broad beans with mustard paste)

Serves four

Ingredients:

Broad bean* – 500 gms

Mustard paste – 2 tbsp

Fenugreek seed – 1 tsp

Turmeric powder/ paste – ½ tsp

Mustard oil – 100 gms

Green chilli – 5 (slit and seeded)

Salt – to taste

* can be replaced with French beans, cauliflowers, brinjals, white radish.

Method:

Wash broad beans and cut in halves. Mix mustard paste in a cup of water. Heat half of the oil in pan, fry fenugreek seeds. Add broad beans and stir for 2 minutes. Add turmeric, chilli and salt, fry. Cover and cook till beans are tender. Now add mustard paste with water and green chillies, cook till done. Add rest of the mustard oil before removing from fire.

⎯⎯⎯⎯ ༄ ⎯⎯⎯⎯

Doi Aalu (potato with yoghurt)

Serves four

Ingredients:

Potato – 300 gms

Yoghurt – 250 gms

Ginger – 2 tsp (finely chopped)

Green chilli – 4 (finely chopped)

Mustard oil – 2 tsp

Salt & sugar – to taste

Method:

Wash and boil potatoes with salt, remove skin. Cut boiled potatoes into slices. Beat yoghurt with sugar. Add potatoes, green chillies, ginger and salt, mix well, taking care not to break the potatoes. Drizzle mustard oil on top and serve cold as a salad.

Doi Chicken (yoghurt chicken)

Ingredients:

Chicken – 1 kg (cut into big pieces)

Yoghurt – 500 gms

Garlic paste – 1 tbsp

Coriander/ methi greens (fresh) – 1 cup

Dried red chilli – 4 (whole)

Peppercorn 8, cinnamon stick 1 ½,

a pod of cardamom

Salt & sugar – to taste

Method:

Mix all the ingredients together, marinate chicken pieces for 30. minutes.

Boil in low heat. No need to add water as usually the yoghurt juice suffices to make the meat tender. Serve with rice or *rotis*.

Machh Bhaja (fried fish Bengali style)

Fish fillets or any other fish can be used.

Ingredients:

Fish – 500 gms (cut into pieces or fillets)

Turmeric powder/ paste – 1 ½ tsp

Ginger paste – 1 tbsp

Onion paste – 2 tbsp

Lemon juice – 1 tbsp

Mustard – 150 gms

Flour – 1/ ½ tbsp

Salt – to taste

Method:

Wash, clean and marinate fish pieces with ginger, garlic, turmeric, salt and lemon juice. Coat the pieces of marinated fish lightly in flour and fry in hot oil. Flip them over till golden brown. Serve with *daal* and rice.

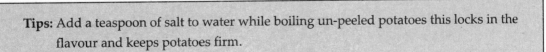

Tips: Add a teaspoon of salt to water while boiling un-peeled potatoes this locks in the flavour and keeps potatoes firm.

Choruibhati

Choruibhatir Maja
– perfect picnics

"*Picnics are a great escape*
On a warm summer day
Butterflies play...
Food to cook and games to play
Picnics are a lot of fun"

– anonymous

Bengali food fetishes are legendary. Darjeeling tea, Hilsa fish, *Golda chingri* and *aalu posto*, top the list. But there is another passion that Bengalis cannot resist. No, not football, cricket, 'dada' (Saurav Ganguly), nor *adda*, it is their wander lust! With dedicated zeal Bengalis research and explore new territories, sample local delights and most of all enjoy sharing experiences over a hearty meal, what else?

There is another aspect about travel, that everyone enjoys even more than the destination itself. It is eating in transit, specially on trains. Most local holidays begin at the Howrah Station. The platforms are the great 'railway bazaars'. Hawkers and peddlers vie for travellers attention. Eager lads jump on to running trains, risking their lives to sell mixed *masala muri*, chips, nuts, chick peas and cold drinks. Food stalls on platforms sell famous local delicacies. One cannot miss Burdwan's *mihidana* (sweet and fine lentil globules) and *sitabhog* (sweets that looks like pilau) or Shaktigarh's *langchas* (cottage cheese dumplings soaked in syrup). Tea is served in terracotta bowls, snacks are served on dried *shaal* leaves. Sadly this tradition of organic crockery is fast disappearing. Often the price of the ticket includes meals. Delhi bound Rajdhani Express offers substantial vegetarian and non-vegetarian meals, which arrive in your own compartment with complimentary bottled water and tea or coffee.

Even ice cream is served as dessert! These meals are available only on certain long distance trains. For shorter overnight journeys most people take along hampers or tiffin carriers. Is it the picnic spirit or fear of being stranded in a god forsaken territory, without food or water that drives people to carry all sorts of eatables? Whatever the reason, it is such fun to open baskets and boxes of food, while precariously balancing plates and spoons on a speeding train! Car journeys too, afford a wonderful opportunity to picnic. Under the shady trees, beside ponds, or paddy fields, amidst a rural setting. Although, spicy hot meals are available at ubiquitous wayside *dhabas* (eateries) on highways, nothing can beat the charm of picnics.

Going down memory lane I remember my childhood days when picnics were an exciting feature of holidays. The idea was to get away from routine, explore nature, have a taste of 'rustic' life and have a jolly time.

TASTES AND SMELLS OF LONG AGO

Long ago, even the journey to Darjeeling was a food adventure. My sister and I, with our parents went up to Darjeeling as soon as summer and the puja holidays began. Those days the train went up to the banks of the river at *Sakrikali Ghat*.

From there we had to board a steamer to cross to *Manihari Ghat*. On board the steamer we ate hot country chicken curry and steaming par boiled rice, cooked by *khalasis* or boatmen. A novelty for us, we found the spicy curries delicious!

Next, an overnight train took us to Siliguri, at the foothills of Darjeeling. Here we boarded the famous toy train, the metre gauge steam locomotive chugged its way up the winding steep mountains to Darjeeling. The queen of hill stations! It was truly an adventure getting there. While on board, the railway waiters would take orders for tea and breakfast at Tindharia, jump off, then magically appear in Tung with a tray of steaming Darjeeling tea. The expert waiters, in maroon turbans and spotless whites trekked up the hilly slopes! At Kurseong, midway to Darjeeling, we would troop out to visit the Waiting Room for a wash, then pop into the dining room to eat a hot breakfast of omlettes and toast served on N E Railway's branded crockery and cutlery, while the Toy train would be refueling with coal and water, letting off steam and waiting for us. The Toy train was enchanting. As it climbed up and up through fog, winding its way through loops and tunnels, the scene would change at every turn. The tropical dense forests, the soaring pines, the giant ferns would be speckled with fluttering butterflies and forest birds The incomparable panorama of the splendid Himalayas unfolded magnificently as we moved along in a gentle pace. The regal pines, the blossomed hill sides, the velvety lichens thick forests and occasional glimpses of the far away silvery snow peaks whetted our appetite for adventure. Darjeeling meant excitement.

A WHIFF OF OLD DARJEELING

The town perched at over 6,500 ft, in the lap of the splendid snow peaks of Kanchenjungha had an air of grace that outmatched every other hill station. Here was a perfect holiday resort. One imbibed the glorious scenery, hobnobbed with friends, took long walks and returned to the sanctuary called home. Our home was 'Malancha', a bower, that father built.

During our stays, either the cook came up with us from Calcutta or mother appointed a local. The meals would be no different from what we were used to at home. Except that we had vegetables that were very local, like 'squash' and greens that were dewy fresh.

We eagerly looked forward to a meal in the town's only Chinese restaurant called The Park, near the Chowrastha or Mall. I found the Egg Fooyong and the Fried Rice most delicious. And there was Pliva, which later changed its

name to Glenary. The whiff of freshly baked batches were irresistible. Lobo's Confectionary, was attended by Mrs Lobo, her cakes and cookies had a home baked delicious flavour which was heavenly. Sometimes mother would ask me to go down and choose the cakes for afternoon tea. What an awesome task, I dithered over my choices... mmm... cream cakes, coconut crunchies, chocolate cookies or a sponge or fruit? Dear Mrs Lobo would gently help me make up my mind.

How can I not mention Keventer's? This food and beverage outlet stocked its own farm and piggery products. Keventer's also served delicious milk shakes and hot chocolates. The rough cut bread, sandwiched with chunky slices

of ham slathered with creamy butter went down well with a cup of hot chocolate or Darjeeling tea. The fried

eggs and sausages were another all time favourite. The best part was to sit on the terrace under the shade of garden umbrellas and feast our eyes on Kanchenjungha.

Another treat we enjoyed as children, were the old fashioned chunky finger chips served with tomato ketchup at

the Gymkhana Club. This was washed down with lemonade or a drink called Vimto! Most refreshing fillers after we skated in the Rink. And a big spoiler of lunch at home, I may add.

The Planter's Club offered English a-la-carte menus for lunch and dinner, which was of indifferent nature. The better hotels such as Everest and Windermere also served meals. The momo eateries (Tibetan dumplings) came up much, much later.

Delicious Bengali sweets, *pantuas*, *rossogollas* and samosas were available at Narayan Das and Indian confectionery shop. But we loved the Puri's Icecreams the most, the hand pushed carts had a sign saying "stop me and buy one" – we utterly loved doing so!

Picnics in the hills....

were delightful and part of our holiday activities. We scrambled up the hills, picked daisies, berries and played in the ferny groves. Red Indians and soldiers, elves and fairies. We chased mini salamanders and butterflies and blew at dandelions to tell the time in fairy land. The elders would sit on a spread sheet, knit and gossip, while we children enjoyed hillside adventures.

The picnics hampers were light and easy to carry, mostly sandwiches and puris and sabzi. oranges and leechis.

....and down in the plains

Car journeys from Kolkata were popular and if one is prepared to risk the traffic these days they can be fun. I remember well, the picnics on long drives on the way to Puri or the jungles of Chotanagpur in Chhatisgarh and Bihar or Jameshedpur started with a game, to locate the right spot. Having found a scenic spot, the hamper would be unpacked and everyone, even the youngest pitched in to help. Beware of carrying uncooked food, in order to have a cook-out in a rustic spot! Once upon a time, a large cauldron of raw meat containing nearly 5 kgs of meat was tucked away in the boot of our car. For a cook – out in a bungalow by the river Ganges. Many cars were loaded with provisions and beer. The four picnickers in one particular vehicle were clearly not aware that a large quantity of uncooked meat was stacked in the boot.

Elaborate instructions were given, on how to get to the 'sylvan' garden house on the banks of the river in Sankrail. The occupants of the car, listened, carefully and made mental notes of all the checkpoints, turns, gullies and signposts. Alas the car never got to the destination. It lost its way! There were no mobile phones those days, the local folks were clueless or perhaps deliberately un-cooperative. In the labyrinth of winding roads and unfamiliar territory, the picnickers were lost. By evening, exhausted, they gave up trying. They headed back to Calcutta and home.

By chance the raw meat was discovered when the 'dicky' was opened to retrieve a duster. Behold there was a huge pot of uncooked meat! Friends waiting on the riverside miles from the city were not amused. They were very cross and very hungry. The picnic turned out to be a disaster, miles from the city, with no food shops in sight and stranded with only raw rice and spices, they cursed the 'lost party' as deliberate spoil sports.

However, all was truly not lost, the 5 kgs of meat was frozen. Next night a delicious and spicy curry was cooked. The picnic turned into a boisterous party.

The meat curry tasted superb, it was washed down with liberal quantities of alcohol. Peace was restored.

Moral of the tale, do not carry uncooked food in case you do not know the way to your destination.

———— THE PERFECT PICNIC BASKET ————

It is best to avoid curries with gravy. Dry vegetables and boneless meat and filleted boneless fish are the safest to carry. The risk of fish bones stuck in the throat in the middle of nowhere is to be avoided. Rice can be messy. Parathaas, luchis and puris made overnight or fresh if time permits are the better option. Buttered slices of bread, boiled eggs and potatoes are filling. Cucumber, capsicum and tomato salads or just a wholesome potato salad with a yoghurt dressing sprinkled with fresh herbs make a hearty make shift meal. Sandesh

or cakes are best desserts. Even better are fresh fruits.

It is important to pack plastic plates, forks, spoons, ground pepper and salt, wet tissues, paper napkins, mosquito repellant, spread sheet, first aid box and games, newspaper, garbage bags to dispose waste.

———— RECIPES ————

Mangsho Bhaja (dry meat/ chicken)

Ingredients:

Meat – 1kg (boneless)

Garlic – 6 cloves (finely chopped)

Ginger – 1" (finely chopped)

Onion – 250 gms (finely chopped)

Green chilli – 2 (slit & seeded)

Dry red chilli – 2 (chopped)

Black pepper corn – 8 (whole)

White oil – 3 tbsp

Vinegar – 1 tbsp

Salt & sugar – to taste

Method:

Boil meat with salt preferably in a pressure cooker, till tender. Drain.

Fry chopped ingredients in a pan, till golden brown. Add the boiled meat and fry till done, add vinegar, sugar and salt to taste. Stir fry till dry.

• Meat may be substituted with boneless chicken.

• Boiled cubed potatoes may be added to increase the quantity. This dry preparation goes well with *parathas* or *luchis*.

———— ◆◆ ————

Meat Chop (meat croquets)

Ingredients:

Meat – 500 gms (minced)

Turmeric powder/ paste – 1 tsp

Red chilli powder/ paste – 1 tsp

Garam masala powder/ paste – 1 tsp

Onion paste – 1 ½ tsp

Ginger paste – 1 tbsp

Garlic paste – 1 tsp

Potato – 500 gms

Egg – 3 (beaten)

Bread crumb – 200 gms

White oil – 300 gms

Salt & sugar – to taste

Method:

Boil minced meat with salt and turmeric. Heat two tbsp oil, add onion, ginger and garlic paste fry till light brown, then add boiled meat, chilli, 1 tsp sugar and salt, sprinkle a little water, fry for 4 minutes, add *garam masala* and stir fry till dry. Remove from fire and keep aside. Beat eggs in a bowl with a little salt and keep aside.

Boil potatoes, peel and mash well. Divide mashed potatoes into 8 to 10 portions. Fill each portion with meat mixture. Seal. Dip each chop into beaten egg and coat with bread crumbs. Deep fry till golden brown.

Easy Shammi Kebab

Serves four

Ingredients:

Minced meat – 500 gms

Chana daal – 200 gms

Ginger – 1 tbsp (chopped)

Garlic – 4 cloves (chopped)

Green cardamom – 3 (seeds only)

Black peppercorn – 6 (whole)

Egg – 2

White oil – 100 gms

Salt – to taste

Method:

Boil together mince meat, *chana daal*, chopped ginger, garlic, salt, cardamom and black peppercorns. Make a fine paste of this boiled mixture in a grinder or by hand in a stone pestle (*sheel-nora*). Add beaten eggs. Make into round balls, flatten them and shallow fry in white oil.

Karaishuti Bhaja (fried green peas)

Serves four

Ingredients:

Green peas – 500 gms (shelled)

Potato – 4 (boiled)

Ginger – 1 tbsp (grated)

Green chilli – 4 (whole)

Fresh coriander leaf – a bunch

White oil – 1 tbsp

Salt – to taste

Method:

Boil green peas. Peel and cube boil potatoes. Fry all ingredients together. Add coriander leaves.

Cool and pack.

*"Be a gentle friend to trees
and they will give you back beauty,
cool and fragrant shade,
and many birds, singing."*

Tips:
To make green bananas ripe in a short time store them with a few lemons in a closed polythene packet.

Parbon

Utshaber Anando

– ceremonies, customs and cuisine

"Bangalir baro mashe tero parbon" *
– a popular Bengali saying

The seasons play a significant role in Bengali rituals. Myths and legends which originated from astrological observations and the cycle of nature are observed with reverence. Ethnic flavour and culture prevail. There is a day to fast, and a day to indulge. There is a day to be vegetarian and a day to eat flesh or fish. Thus throughout the twelve months, because of religious reasons and customs, the menu in most households sees a change. There may be times when the fare is stark, but it is balanced later with superb delicacies in celebration of a ritual.

Bengali New Year's Day (*Nababarsha*), is when Bengalis revel in their Bengali identity and look forward to a hearty and traditional Bengali feast. It is a day to ask for the blessings of Lord Ganesh, the God of prosperity.

Holi, the festival of spring, arrives at the brink of a long, hot approaching summer. The day calls for soothing sherbets. After a frolic and romp with coloured water sprays and abir, (coloured powder) and much merry-making, sweets and cool drinks are very welcome.

In Bengal, even mortals are felicitated with rituals. Special days are marked in the almanac, for the well being of sons-in-law, brothers and mothers-to-be. Even, bachelors and unmarried girls, about to get married, are heartily blessed. The pre-nuptial rituals are incomplete without sumptuous feasts, heartily approved by priests, family and friends alike!

Wedding customs and banquets are the grandest of all. The ritual festivities carry on for weeks. The lavish repasts and rejoicing are replete with indulgence and jollification.

Traditional ceremonial menus, that are relevant to the occasion, have been provided in the following pages. All recipes are in the book.

* "The Bengali almanac has twelve months and thirteen festivals."

— *NABOBARSHO* —
Bengali New Year

Menu

Lunch

Bhaat
(plain rice)

Shukto
(mixed vegetable curry with bitter gourd)

Shona Moog Daal
(split green gram)

Machher Chop
(fish croquets)

Shorshe Pabda
(Indian butter fish in mustard gravy)

Chanar Dalna
(cottage cheese curry)

Mangshor Jhol
(meat stew with spices)

Aamer Chutney
(mango chutney)

Mishti Doi
(sweet yoghurt)

Rosogolla
(sweet cottage cheese balls in syrup)

Dinner

Luchi
(fried flour bread)

Begun Bhaja
(fried brinjal)

Narkel Diye Chholar Daal
(split Bengal gram with coconut)

Kumror Chokka
(red pumpkin with chick peas)

Machh Potoler Dolma
(parval with fish stuffing)

Kasha Mangsho
(dry and spicy meat curry)

Khejur Amshottor Chutney
(date and mango preserve chutney)

Rabri
(milk pudding)

JAMAI SHOSTHI

On this day, in at the height of summer, mothers-in-law, fast for the well being of their *Jamai* (son-in-law) — a very important gentleman. Fortunately the whole family gets to enjoy the glorious feast.

Menu

Breakfast

Luchi	Ghugni	Himsagar Aam
(fried flour bread)	(yellow pea curry)	(himsagar mangoes)
Dumo Dumo Aalu Bhaja	**Lichu**	**Rosogolla**
(fried potato cubes)	(lychees)	(sweet cottage cheese balls in syrup)

Lunch

Option I	Option II
Ghee Bhaat	**Ghee Bhaat**
(bengali pilau)	(bengali pilau)
Narkel Diye Chholar Daal	**Arhar Daal**
(split Bengal gram with coconut	(split pegion pea lentils)
Machh Potoler Dolma	**Topse Fry**
(parval with fish stuffing)	(fried mango fish)
Enchorer Daalna	**Enchorer Daalna**
(green jackfruit curry)	(green jackfruit curry)
Shorshe Pabda	**Doi Machh**
(butter fish in mustard gravy)	(carp with yoghurt)
Mangshor Kalia	**Mangshor Korma**
(rich meat curry)	(exotic meat curry)
Aamer Jhol	**Aamer Chutney**
(green mangoes in sweet & sour syrup)	(mango chutney)
Mishti Doi	**Payesh**
(sweet yoghurt)	(rice pudding)
Soft Sandesh	**Malpoa**
(milk sweets)	(sweet fritters)

Menu

Dinner

Option I	Option II
Parotha	**Luchi**
(fried flatbread)	(fried flour bread)
—••—	—••—
Narkel Diye Chholar Daal	**Ghugni**
(split Bengal gram with coconut)	(yellow pea curry)
—••—	—••—
Begun Bhaja	**Mangsho Bhaat**
(fried brinjal)	(meat pilau)
—••—	—••—
Machher Chop	**Dimer Devil**
(fish croquets)	(deviled egg)
—••—	—••—
Kasha Mangsho	**Anaras Chutney**
(dry and spicy meat curry)	(pineapple chutney)
—••—	—••—
Khejur Amshottor Chutney	**Bhapa Doi**
(date and mango preserve chutney)	(backed youhurt)
—••—	
Rasomalai	
(milk pudding)	

HOLI

In March or April, Holi is celebrated all over India. It is a festival of spring.

In Bengal, the celebration is rather poetic. Rabindranath Tagore's family celebrated not only with flowers but with music as well. The tradition persists. Soirees and concerts, revelry and feasting mark the festival. Holi calls for shorbot and sweets.

Aam Porar Shorbot (raw green mango sherbets)

Serves four

Ingredients:

Raw green mangoes – 2

Sugar – to taste

Black salt or plain salt – 1tsp

Cumin seed – 1 ½ tsp (Roasted and ground finely)

Method:

Roast raw mangoes, if not possible, the mangoes can be boiled, (discard the seeds), peel the skin. The pulp should be soft and mushy, mash the pulp till smooth, add sugar and salt. The ingredients can be blended in a mixer with water. Chill and garnish with the roasted ground cumin seeds.

Ghole (yoghurt drink)

Serves four

Ingredients:

Yoghurt – 1 kg (thick unsweetened)

Sugar – to taste

Rose water or lemon juice – 2 tbsp

Method:

Mix all ingredients in a mixer till the mixture is smooth, add water to your taste and a few drop of rose water or lemon juice. Serve chilled.

Baeler Shorbot (wood apple sherbet)

Serves four

Ingredients:

Wood apple – 1 (large)

Sugar – to taste

Method:

Crack the wood apple and take out the fleshy parts, Boil the flesh and take out the seeds, by straining in a large sieve or muslin cloth. Add sugar, chill and serve. Recommended for stomach problems.

Tormujer Shorbot (watermelon sherbet)

Serves four

Ingredients:

Watermelon – 1 (medium sized)

Sugar – to taste

Method:

Wash and cut watermelon in to wedges. De-seed and peel watermelon wedges, place them in a mixer and blend. Add sugar if necessary. Serve chilled.

Pista Badaamer Shorbot (pistachio or almond sherbet)

Ingredients:

Milk – 1 litre

Pistachio or almond – 100 gms (soaked, peeled and ground)

Sugar – 50gms

Cardamom – 2 (whole and few seeds)

Method:

Boil the milk till it thickens slightly. Add sugar. Mix the nuts. Blend well in a mixer. Chill. Sprinkle ground cardamom seeds before serving.

BHAI PHOTA

The *Bhai Phota* celebration is held two days after Kali *Puja*. It is the day dedicated to brothers. Sisters shower them with affection. A sandalwood spot is put on the brother's forehead by his sister who simultaneously utters a little rhyme praying for his longevity. A lavish feast fit for a king is then served lovingly by the sister.

Menu

Breakfast or tea

Phulkopir Shingara
(cauliflower-vegetable pasties)
—◆◆—

Luchi
(fried flour bread)
—◆◆—

Ghugni
(yellow pea curry)
—◆◆—

Elojhelo
—◆◆—

Patishapta
—◆◆—

Sandesh
—◆◆—

Rosogolla

Lunch or Dinner

Ghee Bhaat
(Bengali pilau)
—◆◆—

Moog Daal
(split green gram)
—◆◆—

Galda Chingrir Matha Bhaja
(fried crayfish head)
—◆◆—

Aalu Potoler Dalna
(potato pumpkin curry)
—◆◆—

Chingri Machher Malai Curry
(prawn in coconut gravy)
—◆◆—

Mangshor Kalia
(rich meat curry)
—◆◆—

Mishti Doi & Rosomalai

— BENGALI WEDDINGS —

As with all Indian weddings, the Hindu Bengali marriage ceremonies are elaborate and extended. The wedding date is set by priests according to a lunar almanac. The ceremonial menus are guided by the availability of seasonal produce. A pre-wedding celebration is the *Gai Holud* and another one *Ay Buro Bhat*. These are equivalent to wedding showers. They are held in the bride or groom's homes, when select friends and relatives are invited for the pre-marriage jollifications. The pre-nuptial bath rituals are followed by a big lunch. These wedding feasts are nowadays generally catered by professional chefs.

Ay Buro Bhat
Menu

Bhaat
(plain rice)

Shukto
(mixed vegetable stew with bitter gourd)

Lau Diye Bhaja Mooger Daal
(roasted split green gram with gourd)

Begun Bhaja
(fried brinjal)

Jhuro Aalu Bhaja
(fried potato juliennes)

Bori Bhaja
(fried lentil ball)

Kumror Phul Bhaja
(pumpkin flower fritters)

Mourala Machh Bhaja
(fried white bait)

Enchorer Daalna
(green jackfruit curry)

Tel Koi
(climbing perch in pungent oil)

Doi Machh
(carp with yoghurt)

Khejur Amshottor Chutney
(date and dried mango chutney)

Misti Doi
(sweet yoghurt)

Rosogolla
(sweet cottage cheese balls in syrup)

Sandesh

Boubhat
Menu

Bhaat & Ghee
(plain rice & clarified butter)
—••—

Moog Daal
(split green gram)
—••—

Jhuro Aalu Bhaja
(fried potato juliennes)
—••—

Topse Fry
(fried mango fish)
—••—

Mocha Ghonto
(banana flower with coconut and potato)
—••—

Ilish Bhapa
(steamed hilsa in mustard gravy)
—••—

Mangshor Jhol
(meat stew with spices)
—••—

Amer/ Anarasher Chutney
(mango/ pineapple chutney)
—••—

Chhanar Payesh
(cottage cheese pudding)

Shaadh

This is the only ceremonial luncheon that is created to please a woman. A woman who is pregnant is indulged by her mother or mother-in-law with a feast a few months before she gives birth. The ritual menu must have several fries, a fish head and rounded off with a ceremonial rice pudding. Meat is not a part of this lunch.

Menu

Bhaat
(plain rice)
—••—

Shukto
(mixed vegetable curry with bitter gourd)
—••—

Lau Diye Bhaja Mooger Daal
(roasted split green gram with gourd)
—••—

Jhuro Aalu Bhaja
(fried potato juliennes)
—••—

Machher Maathaar Muri Ghonto
(fish head with rice and vegetables)
—••—

Rui Machher Kalia
(fish and potato curry)
—••—

Shorshe Pabda
(Indian butter fish in mustard gravy)
—••—

Khejur Amshottor Chutney
(date and mango preserve chutney)
—••—

Payesh
(rice pudding)
—••—

Chandrapuli
(coconut cake)
—••—

Pujo

Pujor Bhojon

— festive fare

By October, the dark monsoon clouds start to disappear. The sun turns mellow and golden, Flashes of blue sky, and feathery clouds herald the arrival of autumn. The joy of anticipation is felt in the air. The fragrant white *shewli* blossoms start to appear and is a sign that Durga is on her way. Durga is the Goddess of victory. She is worshipped for five days. It is the grandest and most magnificent of all festivals in Bengal. The Goddess has ten arms which hold appropriate weapons to slay the wicked demon 'Ashur'. Splendidly arrayed in gorgeous garments and jewels, she rides a fierce lion. Durga's daughters Lakshmi and Saraswati and sons Ganesh and Kartik visit her earthly home with her.

After five days of worship, with piety and pomp, the images are plunged into the Ganges. These five days, Bengal celebrates with unbridled enthusiasm. Gifts are exchanged. New garments are worn. Delicious delicacies are devoured.

Lakshmi, the Goddess of wealth is worshipped ten days later. And on the darkest night of the year, Goddess Kali, the embodiment of power is worshipped. Saraswati, the Goddess of knowledge is worshipped in spring. Blossoms and berries are offered by students and knowledge seekers. There are many pujas to be celebrated, Vishwakarma (the God of 'machines) and Janmashtami, Lord Krishna's birth anniversary, amongst others.

The Bengali almanac has many days set aside for the worship of different deities, corresponding to a particular season. The rituals are varied. Yet the mantra is universal. It teaches us to respect and worship nature. After all, whatever is born of the earth is created with the blessings of heaven.

—— DURGA PUJA ——

Each auspicious day of this religious festival is marked with a set of menus, ranging from pure vegetarian to spicy non-vegetarian fare.

Menu

Ashtami

Lunch	Dinner
Polau (Bengali pilau)	**Luchi** (fried flour bread)
Moog Daal (split green gram)	**Narkel Diye Cholar Daal** (split bengal gram with coconut)
Beguni (brinjal fritters)	**Begun Bhaja** (fried brinjal)
Mochar Ghonto (banana flower with coconut and potato)	**Aalur Saada Torkari** (simple non-spicy potato stew)
Dhokar Dalna (lentil cake curry)	**Chhanar Daalna** (cottage cheese curry)
Misti Doi (sweet yoghurt)	**Khejur Amshottor Chutney** (date and mango preserve chutney)
Tomato Chutney	**Mishti** (assorted traditional Bengali sweets)
Mishti (assorted traditional Bengali sweets)	

Menu

Nabami

Lunch

Bhaat
(plain rice)

Piaj Tomato Diye Daal
(lentils with onion and tomatoes)

Dumo Dumo Aalu Bhaja
(fried potato cubes)

Mochar Ghonto
(banana flower with coconut and potato)

Rui Machher Kalia
(fish and potato curry)

Mangshor Jhol
(meat stew with spices)

Khejur Amshottor Chutney
(date and mango preserve chutney)

Mishti Doi
(sweet yoghurt)

Mishti
(assorted traditional Bengali sweets)

Dinner

Parota
(fried flatbread)

Narkel Diye Cholar Daal
(split bengal gram with coconut)

Begun Bhaja
(fried brinjal)

Maach Potoler Dolma
(parval with fish stuffing)

Kasha Mangsho
(dry and spicy meat curry)

Jalpai Chutney
(olive chutney)

Mishti
(assorted traditional Bengali sweets)

———— LAKSHMI PUJA ————

The *prasad,* or the offerings to her, are autumnal. Pink lotus buds, ripe coconuts, delicately flavoured palm molasses, rice, *khoi, chirey* (varieties of puffed rice), *mowas, murki* (or traditional sweets), *kheer* or milk and bananas, also *khichuri.*

Menu

Dinner

——— ৯৫ ———

Khichuri

(kedgeree)

— •• —

Begun Bhaja

(fried brinjal)

— •• —

Luchi

(fried flour bread)

— •• —

Phulkopir Daalna

(cauliflower curry)

Kumror Chhokka

(red pumpkin with chick peas)

— •• —

Jalpai Chutney

(olive chutney)

— •• —

Mishti

(assorted traditional Bengali sweets)

———— KALI PUJA ————

Mother *Kali* is the all-powerful deity of Bengal. She may look intimidating, but Bengalis believe that she has the most forgiving and loving heart, bestowing her blessings on all those who pray to her. On the dark night before *"Kali Puja"*, it is customary to light fourteen lamps and eat fourteen varieties of *shaak* (spinach) to ward off the evil spirits. There may be some homespun wisdom in this, as the *shaks* constitute edible weeds and leafy shrubs - a practical form of weeding!

Bhog/ offerings

——— ৯৫ ———

Khichuri	**Panch Mishali Charchchari**	**Payesh**
(kedgeree)	(stir fried vegetables)	(rice pudding)
— •• —	— •• —	— •• —
Luchi	**Bhaja**	**Mishti**
(fried flour bread)	(assorted fries)	(assorted Bengali sweets)

─── *SARASWATI PUJA* ───

Saraswati is the Goddess of knowledge and learning and also of spring. This lovely *vasant panchami* spring day is the day is for eating *khichuri* or kedgeree, and savour the tart-sweet *kool* (Indian plum) which is made into an irresistible sweet and sour chutney. This is a delicious accompaniment to the *khichuri*. Some will even add the first *ilish* or hilsa of the season to the menu, which was taboo throughout winter. Saraswati puja is celebrated mostly by students and youngsters.

In West Bengal, *'gota'* is a traditional delicacy enjoyed at this time. The *'gota'* is an all-in-one dish. Whole black lentils or *kalai* beans are soaked, boiled with salt, ginger and aniseed paste and six types of uncut and unpeeled, whole vegetables, such as baby new potatoes, brinjals, red potatoes, green peas, radish, spinach shoots and green chillies. This delicious stew is kept aside over night and enjoyed the next day with pungent mustard oil drizzled over it.

Menu

Lunch (veg)	Lunch (non-veg)
Bhuni Khichuri	**Khichuri**
(dry kedgeree)	(kedgeree)
Beguni	**Bokphul Bhaja**
(brinjal fritters)	(sesbania flower fritters)
Kumrorphul Bhaja	**Ilishmach Bhaja**
(pumpkin flower fritters)	(fried hilsa)
Sish Paalang Charchchari	**Ilish MachherTauk**
(spinach shoots fry)	(hilsa sour)
Kooler Chutney	**Payesh**
(Indian plum chutney)	(rice pudding)
Payesh	**Sandesh**
(rice pudding)	(traditional Bengali sweets)
Mishti	
(traditional Bengali sweets)	

———— MONSOON RITUALS ————

Rath Jatra, Lord Jagannath's chariot festival, is celebrated during the rains. Other monsoon festivals are *Janmashtami, Tal Nabomi, Ranna Puja* and *Bishwakarma Puja.*

Sweets such as *tal* (palmyra fruit) fritters and coconut balls are eaten on *Janmashtami,* the birthday of Lord Krishna. The recipe has not changed from ancient times. In the *'Baishnab Padabali',* (a lyrical ode to Lord Krishna), Radha sings in praise of the palmyra fruit: *"Tomal kalo, Krishna kalo, taito tomal lage bhalo"* (The palmyra fruit is black and so is Krishna, which is why I like palmyra fruit).

Ranna Puja and *Bishwakarma Pujas* are held when the monsoons are tapering off. Though it is called *Ranna* (cooking) *Puja,* it is a day when nothing is cooked at all!

A rural ritual, a meal comprising greens and hilsa fish is prepared and stored away to be eaten the next day. Why eat stale food? Because even the stove and the cook deserve a holiday!

Bishwakarma, the lord of machines is worshipped by mechanics — and by everyone else who uses computers! A lip-smacking meal of rice and mutton curry (invariably washed down with rum), follows after reverential prayers.

Biswakarma Puja heralds the end of the rains but a balmy breeze sweeps the sky. It's a fun day when the old and young participate in a battle of kites.

To capture the flavour of old times, here are some of those near-forgotten recipe.

———— RECIPE ————

Serves four

Taler Bora (palmyra-fruit fritters)

Ingredients:

Palmyra fruits (*tal*) – 1 (ripe)

Coconut (fresh) – ½ (grated)

Sugar – to taste

Wheat flour – to bind

Oil – 250 gms

Method:

Remove skin from fruit. Separate seeds. To extract the pulp, use a *'tal ghosuni'* or even rub the fruit against a clean cane basket or grater.

Combine the pulp with the coconut, wheat flour and sugar. The amount of sugar will vary according to the sweetness of the fruit. Heat oil and drop balls of the mixture into it.

Fry the fritters till brown.

Tal Kheer (palmyra fruit pudding)

Ingredients:

Palmyra fruit – 2 (ripe)

Milk – 1 litre

Coconuts – 2 (grated)

Sugar – to taste

Method:

Remove skin from fruit. Separate seeds. To extract the pulp, use a *'tal ghosuni'* or even rub the fruit against a clean cane basket or grater.

Put the pulp in clean cloth and hang up for an hour for the juice to drain out.

Boil the milk till thickened. Add the fruit pulp, coconut and sugar and simmer, taking care as the boiling fruit might splatter. Cook till the mixture takes on a dark tinge.

• This can be eaten by itself or with popped rice *(muri)*.

Ilish Machher Matha Diye Kochur Shaak

(taro stalks with hilsa head)

Ingredients:

Taro stalk – 2 bundles

Hilsa head – 2 (washed and cleaned)

Oil – 2 tbsp

Onion seed – 1 tsp

Turmeric powder/ paste – 1tsp

Green chilli – 4 (slit and seeded)

Salt – to taste

Method:

Smear hilsa head with a pinch of turmeric and keep aside. Cut the taro stalks into 2" pieces and remove the skin. Boil the stalks and drain, mash the boiled stalks. Strain out any remaining liquid. Heat oil, fry hilsa head and remove. Add onion seeds and 2 green chillies in the same oil, fry, then add mashed taro stalks, turmeric and salt fry for 3 – 4 minutes. Break hilsa head and add to the pan with green chillies, fry for another three minutes. Remove from fire.

Panchmishali

— miscellaneous

cook by fluke

It was 1pm in the after
when six of us scrambled
a bus in the middle of th
wilderness. We had arr
Joshipur, a small town i
My friends and I wer
way to Simlipal forest.
planned an overnight
Simlipal Tiger Reserve
Joshipur we would hir
and drive to the he
dense forest. This
last stop for stock
provisions. The for
was situated in th
formidable forest
nothing edible to

Thakurbarir Heshel

– traditional cuisine

Rabindranath Tagore (1861-1941) the poet laureate of Bengal was born in his ancestral home in Jorasanko, Kolkata. A recipient of the prestigious Nobel Prize, Tagore is revered as a Guru or prophet in Bengal. He is Bengal's lark and laureate who epitomizes the essence of Bengali culture. He wrote anthologies of essays, poems, novels, dramas and composed a multitude of lyrics and set them to music. He was an avid and acclaimed painter as well. In other words, Tagore was an unparalleled genius, a self realized poet and an exalted soul.

Perhaps all this is common knowledge, what is little known, is his interest in culinary pursuits. Fortunately, the Tagores were prolific writers, and from their biographies and memoirs, glimpses of the poet's gastronomic tastes can be pieced together.

The Tagores were enormously wealthy and not surprising had expensive habits. They were accustomed to a life of luxury. Family dramas and concerts were a part of this lavish setting. Art, poetry and music flourished. Beauty and a fine sense of aesthetics prevailed in all things.

Tagore himself was fastidious about what he wore and how he looked. Tagore was also particular about food. His love of fine food is evident from his writings. He was a prolific writer of novels, essays and poems. His poem, 'Bhojon Bir' is a satire on the 'valiant' Bengali glutton.

"Small portions won't please Damodar Sheth

Fetch big balls of sweets, and fried bhetki

Shoes from Cuttack, and a large pot of ghee

Wriggling fresh perch from Jalpaiguri

And Boaal fish belly from Chandni!

Add to the list China bazzar's berry

Crab's eggs and piping hot tea

For prestige's sake spend freely!

Remember this well, he is quite portly

You'll need large portions note carefully

By the way, what's the going rate

of Jharia's jeelipi?"

— *Damodar Sheth* by Rabindranath Tagore

— GLIMPSES OF THE OLD WORLD —

Jorasanko was Rabindranath's ancestral home. Here he grew up, got married, set up home and lived most of his life. From his well documented biographies the reader gets a vivid picture of life and times in late 19th century and early 20th at Joransanko. Amongst the faded photographs that remain there is one which is of particular interest. It shows Tagore having a meal, seated on the floor with the other invitees as was the custom. The women of the house are seen serving. A gracious touch indeed, for a rich family with many servants. The poet liked his meals to be served aesthetically. Lunch was served on immaculate, white, marble plates. Fine and fragrant rice was heaped in the middle of the plate. Bowls of side dishes containing four or five vegetable preparations and fries

were arranged neatly around the rice. The gleaming brass or black stone bowls of *daal*, fish curries and stewed items were placed around the large marble plate. A variety of savoury items, fish and meat preparations was served. The hearty and carefully cooked meal ended with a piquant sweet sour relish. For Rabindranath, this was an essential finale to the repast. In fact no *Thakurbari* meal was complete without a chutney.

Dinner was another elaborate affair. In contrast to lunch, dinner at Joransanko was served on fine bone china plates. A salad was 'de rigueur', mango or papaya chutneys were also prepared. English puddings, kheer or payesh (rice pudding) were specially cooked by the women of the house. It is interesting to note, from Amita Devi's memoirs, (she was Rabindranath's elder brother's wife) that, the poet liked his salads and was fond of celery. He also liked lentil soup. He enjoyed hot toast with honey and a glass of milk at breakfast. In his childhood auto-biography the poet says, he went for long walks in the hills with his father after downing a hot glass of milk.

Large quantities of milk were delivered daily at Joransanko from the nearby Tagore estates. Gallons of milk were turned into clarified butter or ghee. Despite the generous use of ghee much was left over and thrown away! The wastage of ghee and milk was actually commented upon by some family members with disapproval.

The aristocratic ladies of the house lent a helping hand. The keys to the stores were in their safekeeping. Rations were measured, weighed and doled out. Mounds of vegetables were cut and chopped. This chore was also handled willingly by the ladies of the house. The method of cutting vegetables for each item, required expertise and art. There was yet another chore. Betel leaves (*Paans*) had to be carefully prepared. Each gentleman of the house had his particular choice of *paan* leaf and aromatic fillings. (*Paan* is a flavoury heart shaped leaf, which is made into a triangular envelope, filled with a mixture of betel nut, cardamom seeds, cloves, scented aniseeds etc and chewed at the end of a meal to help digestion). Ornamental *paan* boxes were packed with care and sent to each scion's apartment.

——— JESSORE COMES TO JORASANKO ———

Dwaraknath, Tagore's grandfather, set a tradition of selecting daughters-in-laws, from the district of Jessore. It was a belief that Jessore girls grew up to be perfect housewives. Many brides came to Joransanko from Jessore. They were carefully chosen from good Brahmin families and scrutinized before final wedding arrangements were made. Once the girls entered the Tagore family, they were groomed and taught to take over household duties. Rabindranath's wife, Mrinalini was born in Jessore. She was not only skilled in household chores but was an excellent cook as well. Rabindranath himself, his sister-in-law Ganadanandini Devi and others, travelled to Jessore to select his bride. Mrinalini Devi was the chosen one. Mrinalini, at the age of nine, entered Joransanko as a bride. She took over kitchen duties and learnt much from her mother-in-law. She was admitted to an English school, Rabindranath wanted her to be studious as well as accomplished. Within a few years she took up her duties as a Jorasanko wife. She became an expert housewife, taking care of a large household while bringing up her children as well. She proved to be an excellent cook. Rabindranath himself encouraged Mrinalini to experiment and innovate. Whenever there were social gatherings at home, the poet requested her to cook something special. Nothing common place would do. "There should be nothing ordinary each item should be unique." Mrinalini never failed him, sometimes when he took up the cook's role, Mrinalini stepped in to complete the job. In later years, Tagore himself guided Mrinalini and together they experimented. She had established herself as an unsurpassable cook and thus helped to strengthen the belief that wives from Jessore were truly superior.

Perhaps because of the influence of Jessore, '*Choi*' a spicy, peppery root, was liberally used in both Joransanko and Pathuriaghat (another branch of the Tagores) kitchens. This was a Jessore trait. What red, hot chillies were to Chittagong cuisine, a touch of sweetness to West Bengal's savoury preparations — *choi* was to Jessore and Jorasanko.

——— KITCHEN TALES ———

From Tagore descendants, family memoirs and historical documents, a vivid picture of the life and times of late 19th and early 20th century cuisine of Bengal emerges. These legacies reveal interesting tidbits of the eating habits and customs of the famous Tagores.

The Tagore family enjoyed simple *'bhates'* like brinjal *bharta*. They also liked *chhokkas* and many seasonal vegetable items. Coriander and mint and ginger/mango roots were used for chutneys. Even white gourd, cucumber *raitas* and salads featured in the menu. Fine *Kaminibhog* rice eaten with something bitter as a starter. Followed by a fried item, *ghonto, charchchari*, (vegetable pot-pourri), fish *jhol* or *kalia* (curry). At dinner, puffy wafer thin *luchis* or light hand made *rotis* (bread made with wheat) were accompanied with side dishes of *chhokka*, fries, meat curry and the 'must have' chutney. These elaborate menus were everyday fare for the Tagores.

Another lady of the household, who cooked lovingly for Rabindranath, was his grand niece-in-law Amita Devi (the poet's elder brother Dwijendranth's grand daughter-in-law), Very talented, and accomplished, Amita Devi was an actress par excellence. She was loved and regarded by the poet, and she reciprocated with tender, loving care.

It is said that Amita Devi, nurtured a rather unwell Rabindranath to health with her ingenious preparations. She made delicious *'kalai' daal*, with the aromatic *Gandharaj* lime. She cooked *Pabda* fish with fresh coriander which the poet ate with relish. Was it then that a tradition was set? Now *Pabda* fish cooked with coriander is a popular combination. Tender goat meat curry made with asafeotida, coriander and cumin, garnished with roasted cuminseed powder was specially prepared for the Poet by Amita Devi. Tagore enjoyed the gravy so much he sipped it straight from his bowl and no doubt recovered fast.

Talking of food, one must mention a few of the other Tagore family ladies who took culinary skills to greater heights. One such lady was Pragya Sundari Devi, daughter of Hemendranath Tagore, married to Lakshminath BejBarua. She has to be credited for creating new dishes, writing down recipes with correct measurements. She contributed her recipes to local journals and introduced the word 'menu' to Bengalis. The other ladies of the Tagore family who left their mark in the history of Bengali cuisine are, Nalini Devi and her daughter Purnima Devi. Related to the poet Rabindranath through both Joransanko and Pathuria-ghat lineage. Purnima Devi has written a comprehensive and interesting recipe book called *"Thakur Barir Ranna"*. The recipes were bequeathed to her by her mother and by Indira Devi, daughter of the Poet's elder brother Satyandranath and Gyanadanandini Tagore. Indira Devi was an enthusiastic collector of recipes. She travelled all over the world.

Although she did not cook herself, she was a food enthusiast and very modern in her views. Whenever she came across an interesting preparation, Indira Devi noted it down. The recipes were scribbled in tattered sheets more like daily household *hisabs* (accounts), according to Purnima Devi.

While on the subject of old Bengali recipes, mention must be made of Bipradas Mukhopadhay. A famous actor and dramatist (1842-1914) He wrote a significant recipe book called '*Pak Pranali*'. The recipes are the most authentic. His cooking tips and instructions may seem archaic and amusing today, but the book is a tome of Bengali cuisine. The recipes in this chapter are gathered from the past and made simple for present day use.

—— RECIPES ——

Shol Machher Aamjhol (shol/ murrel fish with raw mango) | Serves four

Ingredients:

Shol (murrel) – 500 gms

Mustard oil – 4 tbsp

Panch phoron – 1 tsp (whole), ½ tsp (powdered)

Raw mango – 3 tbsp (finely sliced)

Turmeric powder/ paste – 2 tsp

Green chilli – 4 (slit & seeded)

Salt & sugar – to taste

Method:

Fry fish and remove bones. Fry *panch phoron*, add raw mango slices. Season with salt. When mangos are tender, add fish and turmeric. Cook over low heat for 10 minutes. Add sugar, water and green chillies, cover and simmer. When the gravy thickens, add *panch phoron* powder. This tangy broth is delicious and ideal for hot summer days.

• A mix of fenugreek, fennel and cumin seeds may be substituted for the *panch phoron*.

Maccher Torkari (fish with vegetables)

| Serves four

Ingredients:

Rui (carp) – 500 gms (large pieces)

Mustard seed – 2 tsp

Panch phoron – 2 tsp

Brinjal – 200 gms

Ridge gourd – 200 gms

Turmeric powder/ paste – 2 tsp

Green chilli – 2 (slit & seeded)

Red chilli powder/ paste – 1 tsp

Ginger paste – 2 tsp

Salt – to taste

Method:

Fry fish. Flake and remove bones. Roast and grind mustard and *panch phoron* seeds. Dice vegetables. Heat oil, fry green chillies and ground spice. Fry vegetables and fish flakes. Add turmeric, red chilli, salt and a cup of water. Simmer, it should be moist, not watery, lastly add the ginger paste.

- Carp can be substituted with, shrimps, *koi* (climbing perch), or *magur* (cat fish).
- Coriander and bay leaf pastes were sometimes added for extra flavour and aroma.

Mouralar Bati Charchchari (steamed mola carplet with mustard)

Ingredients:

| Serves four

Mourala fish – 250 gms (sprats)

Mustard oil – 4 tbsp

Onion – 2 (chopped)

Green chilli – 2 (slit & seeded)

Mustard paste – 2 tbsp

Turmeric powder/ paste – 3 tsp

Salt – to taste

Method:

Clean and wash fish and mix with all other ingredients. Add about a cup of water, cover and cook over low heat till water has been absorbed.

- Can also be steamed by placing the vessel in a larger pan of boiling water.
- Shrimp and hilsa fish may be cooked this way.

Tips: Rub your hands with oil before chopping vegetables, to keep stains out and softness in.

Lau Posto (gourd with poppy seeds)

Ingredients:

Gourd – 1 kg (chopped in small pieces)

Dried lentil balls (*bori*) – 50 gms
(fried and broken)

Dried red chilli – 3 (whole)

Poppy seed paste – 4 tbsp

Ginger paste – 3 tsp

Mustard oil – 3 tbsp

Ghee – 1 tsp

Salt & sugar – to taste

Method:

Fry the gourd (if too hard. then steam first). Add red chilli, ginger and poppy seed pastes, lower the flame, there is no need to add water at this stage. When the vegetables are cooked add fried *boris*, salt and sugar. Sprinkle water, cover and cook till done. Before taking it off the fire, add the ghee.

• Along with the bottle gourd, its stems and tender leaves can also be used.

Dhonepata Diye Mangsho (meat in coriander gravy)

Ingredients:

Chicken/ meat – 1 kg

yoghurt – 500 gms (beaten)

Garlic paste – 5 tbsp

Ginger paste – 3 tbsp

Coriander leaf – 6 tbsp (paste)

Green chilli paste – to taste

Ghee or white oil – ½ cup

Salt & sugar – to taste

Method:

Marinate meat in the mixture of yoghurt, ginger, garlic, coriander and chilli pastes for 2 hours. Add salt. Heat oil and pour marinated meat. Stir fry.

Cover and cook, stirring from time to time and sprinkling water if necessary. When the meat is tender, add sugar and cook uncovered till the water is absorbed.

• Mutton can be pressure-cooked and then left to simmer till the gravy is of desired thickness.

Tips: To boil meat quickly add raw papaya paste to the curry. Marinate meat before cooking in a mixture of ginger, garlic and raw papaya paste to make the meat very tender.

Potoler Malai Curry (parval in coconut gravy)

Ingredients:

Potol (parval) – 1 kg (large size)
Potato – 500 gms
Coconut (fresh) – 1 (medium)
Asafoetida – a pinch
Garam masala – 3 cloves, 3 cardamoms, cinnamon 1" (whole)
Red chilli powder/ paste – to taste
Ginger paste – 4 tsp
Turmeric powder/ paste – 4 tsp
Yoghurt – ½ cup
Mustard oil – 150 gms
Ghee – to garnish
Salt & sugar – to taste

Method:

Peel *potols* (parvals), keep them whole. Peel and quarter the potatoes. Scrape flesh from coconut and grind to a paste.

In hot oil, fry asafoetida, whole *garam masala*, red chilli, ginger and turmeric. Add yoghurt, potatoes and *potols*. Stir well. Add the coconut paste, salt, sugar and a little water, cover and cook till done. Garnish with ghee before taking it off the fire.

Pui Dantar Charchchari (vegetables with greens)

Ingredients:

Pui greens and stalk – 500 gms
Potato – 200 gms
Broad bean – 100 gms
Brinjal & Sweet potato – 200 gms each
Red pumpkin – 150 gms
Horse radish – 200 gms
Mustard oil – 5 tbsp
Panch phoron – ½ tsp
Red chilli powder/ paste – 2 tsp (optional)
Mustard paste – 2 tbsp
Turmeric powder/ paste – 1 tbsp
Green chilli – 2 (slit) & Salt – to taste

Method:

Chop the greens. Cut all vegetables into thin strips, the brinjal and pumpkin pieces should be slightly larger than the rest, so that they do not become over cooked. Heat oil fry *panch phoron* and green chillies. Add potatoes, fry, then put rest of the vegetables. Cover and simmer, stir and sprinkle water and fry till vegetables are tender. Add turmeric, salt, mustard and red chilli pastes. Cook till done and water has been absorbed.

> • Shrimp or head of hilsa fish can be added in this recipe.

Magur Machher Hingi (Indian catfish with asafoetida)

Serves four

Ingredients:

Magur (cat fish) – 4 (halved)

Potato – 200 gms

Potol – 200 gms

Raw banana – 1 (large)

Turmeric paste/ powder – 2 tsp

Groundnut oil – 2 tbsp

Mustard seed – 2 tbsp

Coriander seed – 2 tsp

Cumin seed – 2 tsp

Asafoetida – a pinch

Garam masala – 1 tsp

Milk – 1½ tbsp

Salt & sugar – to taste

Method:

Peel and cut vegetables into cubes. Fry and keep aside. Smear fish with turmeric and salt. Fry and keep aside. Grind to a paste mustard, coriander and cumin seeds. Add ¾ cups of water to the spice paste and simmer. Add vegetables, cover and simmer till vegetables are tender. Then add fish, salt, sugar and cook till the gravy thickens. Heat a little oil in another pan to lightly temper the asafoetida and add it to the fish stew. Sprinkle with *garam masala* powder and lastly stir in milk. This is known as *'gola hingi'* and it goes very well with rice in summer, Ideal for lunch. The *'kosha hingi'* is a richer variation, in which the spice paste is fried with curd and onion paste. The gravy is thicker.

Panthar Mangsho Ba Murgir Rassala (goat meat or chicken rezala)

Use the same recipe for Goat Meat or Chicken

Serves four

Ingredients:

Chicken/ meat – 1 kg

Yoghurt – 500 gms (beaten)

Onion – 500 gms (chopped)

Garlic paste – 2 tbsp

Green chilli – 4 (slit)

Bay leaf – 3 or 4

Red chilli powder/ paste – 1 tsp

Ghee or groundnut oil – 500 gms

Salt & sugar – to taste

Method:

Marinate the meat pieces for four hours in curd combined with other ingredients. Simmer in a covered vessel, stirring from time to time, adding water when necessary.

Cook till meat is tender, the gravy is thick and the oil floats to the top.

Jhinger Ghonto (ridge gourd with coconut)

Ingredients:

Ridge gourd – 1 kg

Coconut (fresh) – 1 (small)

Ginger – 1" (shreded)

Dried lentil ball (bori) – 50 gms

Groundnut oil – 4 tbsp

Green chilli – 4 (slit & seeded)

Bay leaf – 4

Cumin seed – 2 tsp

Coriander powder/ paste – ½ tbsp

Cumin powder/ paste – ½ tbsp

Milk – 3 tbsp

Flour – 1½ tbsp

Salt & sugar– to taste

Method:

Cut gourd into small pieces. Scrape flesh from coconut. Fry *boris* and crush. Heat oil and put in the bay leaves, chillies and cumin seeds. When spices are slightly cooked add gourd, with coriander and cumin. Stir till cooked. Add salt, cover and simmer. When gourd is tender, uncover to let the water evaporate.

Stir in grated coconut with sugar. Next, mix flour and milk and add to the pan. When gravy is thick, sprinkle with crushed *boris*.

- This preparation is meant to be slightly sweet.
- Thinly-sliced potato can be used together with the gourd.
- Rub the serving dish with a slice of lime before placing vegetable in it. The fragrance will add a flavour to the dish.
- Another variation is to use asafoetida. Roast the asafoetida with a bit of cumin seed powder and add to the recipe.

———— 🙟 ————

Chinrer Payesh (flattened rice dessert)

Ingredients:

Milk – 500 ml

Flattened rice – 125 gms

Sugar – to taste

Raisins – a handful

Black cardamom powder – 1 tsp

Method:

Boil and thicken the milk. Add the washed flattened rice. When the flattened rice is cooked slightly add the sugar and raisins. Sprinkle with cardamom powder.

Slivers of almond can be added.

Cook by Fluke

It was one pm in the afternoon when six of us scrambled out of a bus in the middle of wilderness. We had arrived in Joshipur, a small town in Orissa. My friends and I were on our way to Simlipal Tiger Reserve. We planned an overnight stay at Kairakacha. At Joshipur we would hire a jeep and drive to the heart of the forest. This was also the last stop for stocking up on food provisions. There was nothing edible to be had there – not even a pinch of salt!

We were all hungry, and had delicious lunch at a 'Pice' hotel (cheap eatery). Rice, *daal*, fried potatoes, cauliflower *charchchari* and *parshe* fish *jhol*. It was a hearty meal.

Meanwhile, quite a few chores had to be completed before we set off. A jeep had to be hired for our trip, Mitu and Biswanathda were given the task of organising a jeep. Kushal and Kalyanda were to get the permission from the Tiger Project Office, Raja and I were to buy the food provisions, We set off briskly. Chores done, we planned to meet in front of a hotel.

Our shopping list was formidable. It took us quite a while to get back to the meeting place, the others looked impatient and irritated!

"What took you so long? We have to go to Chahala to pick up the Chowkidar, he has the key to the Kairakacha bungalow." said Kalyanda. Finally, we got the key and the key person and started on a perilous jeep journey. Forested hillsides, giant leafy trees and uneven terrain made the journey slow and precarious. To my horror the jeep was rolling down a slope, I looked down there below was a deep gorge! Horrifying – it was getting darker by the minute. The sun had not set, but the headlights were switched on, the forest was so dense, no natural light filtered through!

—— THE JUNGLE BUNGLE ——

We arrived at Kairakacha. The bungalow looked completely desolate. Wooden planks had to be placed across a ditch that led to the bungalow. After we had crossed over, the planks were withdrawn. This was a precaution against straying wild animals. The condition of the bungalow was deplorable! To top it there was no electricity. Mercifully we had not forgotten the candles! What a mess we were in! The sun had set. Who would have thought it would take us so long to unload the luggage? It was 7.30 pm, party time for our wild friends of the forest. Besides we were all hungry after our rough and jerky ride.

Hunger pangs were causing unbelievable commotion. Lunch had been digested hours ago! Cries of "we want chappatis, we have everything, Debashis you did the shopping now you do the cooking." Someone had to take charge. I set to work, "no *rootis* or *chapattis*, no frills and curries. You will eat what I rustle up!"

I requested Raja to light the stove. Kalyanda murmured hopefully "Rice with egg curry?" I replied "not a chance... be grateful if you get a gruel of some sort", I said.

—— MEN AT WORK ——

Swiftly I fumbled and got a packet of rice, washed and boiled it. Plain boiled rice had to be eaten with something! With what? That was the question. I had a brainwave. Somehow I fished out onions, a few runner beans, half of a cauliflower and cabbage, few broad beans, carrots and a packet of butter from the bag. Raja chopped the vegetables in small bits.

With all these ingredients a wholesome rice dish was made. The bungalow was filled with a delicious aroma. (see recipe in the next page)

—— FOOD GLORIOUS FOOD ... AND? ——

Everyone rushed to the kitchen, to heap their plates with this simple welcome dish. Conversation came to a stop. The silence of the jungle was broken by the clattering of forks, spoons and occasional noises like 'mmmm' 'delicious'. As we walloped this innovative dish hungrily. Suddenly, Kushal alerted us, 'listen' he said. We heard a tiger roaring. Being wild life enthusiasts we ignored our growling stomachs and ran in search of the growling tiger! But not before making a mental note... that amidst wild surroundings a new, unconventional recipe was born... I am happy to share with you some more of those impromptu recipes.

"*Tiger tiger burning bright,
In the forest of the night*"

– William Blake

—— RECIPES ——

Chinchir Polau

Serves eight

Ingredients:

Rice – 500 gms

Onion – 3 large

Bean – 150 gms

Cabbage – ½ of a medium one

Cauliflower – ½ of a medium one

Carrot – 150 gms

Butter – 100 gms

Green chilli – 4 (slit and seeded)

Peppercorn – 2 tsp (whole)

Salt & sugar – to taste

Method:

Wash vegetables. Cut cauliflower into small florets. Chop other vegetables finely. Wash and boil rice, drain and spread to dry. Heat butter in deep pan, add whole peppercorns and finely chopped vegetables. Stir fry for 2 minutes with sugar and salt, add green chillies. Now add cooked rice on low heat, stir and mix well. Serve hot.

Doi Murgi (chicken in yoghurt mustard gravy)

Serves five

Ingredients:

Country chicken – 750 gms

Onion – 3 medium (200 gms)

Garlic – 4 cloves

Ginger paste – 2 tsp

Turmeric paste – 1 tsp

Green chilli – 6 slit and seeded

Peppercorn – 2 tsp (whole)

Mustard seed – 25gms

Yoghurt – 200gms

Mustard oil – 50gms

Lime juice – 1 tbsp

Salt & sugar – to taste

Method:

Soak mustard seeds in water and grind to a paste with a pinch of salt and 2 green chillies. Peel and chop onions, ginger and garlic finely. Add turmeric paste and sugar in yoghurt and beat well. Marinate chicken in the yoghurt mixture for one hour. Heat oil in a pan, add whole peppercorns, onion, ginger and garlic, fry till soft, add marinated chicken, cover the pan and simmer for 20 minutes. Now add mustard paste with a little water, stir well, add in the green chillies, cover and cook till done. Remove from fire.

Dimloo

Ingredients:

Egg – 6 (hard boiled)

Potato – 6 (medium)

Onion – 2 (medium)

Green chilli – 4 (slit and finely chopped)

Peppercorn – 10 (whole), 1 tsp(powdered)

Sunflower oil – 1 ½ tbsp

Butter – 1 tbsp

Salt – to taste

Method:

Boil potatoes, then peel and cut into halves. Shell hard boiled eggs. Peel and chop onions finely. Heat oil in a pan, fry eggs and potatoes separately till light brown, remove and keep aside. Pour more oil in the pan; add whole peppercorns and chopped onions, fry till soft. Add eggs and potatoes fry lightly and add green chillies and salt. Fry another 2 minutes, now add peppercorn powder, butter and salt. Mix well and remove from fire. It goes well with *chapattis* or rice.

Junglee Tea

Ingredients:

Tea – 3 tsp (CTC)

Milk powder – 3 tbsp

Sugar – 3 tsp

Ginger – 2 tsp (grated)

Peppercorn – 4 - 5 (whole)

Water – 4 ½ cup

Salt – a pinch

Method:

Boil water with powdered milk, ginger and peppercorn. Add tea and boil for half minute, add sugar and salt, stir. Remove from fire. Strain and serve hot.

Tips: To open the lid of a new glass bottle, keep it in a bowl containing boiling water for 3-4 minutes. The lid will open easily.

Benglish Cuisine

– colonial influences

At home, when my sister and I were growing up, our meals were divided into two distinct parts. Lunch was always Bengali fare, while dinner was invariably 'English'.

Both meals were cooked by a Barooah Mug cook. (Chitagonians had a reputation of good culinary skills learnt from British *memsahibs*). He was supervised by our mother.

We were served at the dining table by the bearer, while our *ayah* (maid) watched over us to ensure every mouthful was consumed. Our terrier, Kooty, hovered around under the table eagerly for scraps. We delighted in feeding him unwanted bits from our plates so that our meal would finish faster.

Occasionally we rebelled against the bland Western food. Sadly, we only came to appreciate the cook's abilities when we grew up. By then, the breed of *baburchis* had disappeared from Calcutta.

Dinner menus were planned to please our father. *Baba*, as we called him, graduated from Glasgow University, and having spent several years in Scotland, he enjoyed Western cuisine. I recall vividly the dinner menus, which consisted of a soup, and a main course of fish or meat served with boiled vegetables, and a pudding to follow.

I look back and marvel at the ingenuity of the *Baburchi's* skills! Born in a remote village of Bengal, with practically no knowledge of English, and with few implements and even fewer ingredients, the cooks conjured wonderful puddings and entrees.

The recipes were handed down by word-of-mouth. One thing there was no shortage of was city gas! And a cleverly constructed smokeless stove in our home in Darjeeling was the source of many splendid meals! Hot water was never a problem. So vital was the role of the cook in the Majumdar house-hold that he even travelled with us to Darjeeling where we went to escape Calcutta's summer heat.

Although this book is devoted to Bengali cuisine, I cannot help but recapture some of the 'English' delights from our Bengali *'baburchi khana'*.

As a child I spent many evenings watching Simon Gomes, the cook, carve flowers from cucumbers, carrots and tomatoes. My particular favourite was the sugar basket moulded from caramelized sugar, complete with a braided handle and filled with fresh cream and fruits.

Baked custards, bread puddings, smooth custards served with stewed fruit or apricots and lemon soufflé were every-day food! Mutton roasts, brown stews, Irish stews, crumbed lamb chops, glacé, shepherd's pie, mutton potato chops, fish mayonnaise, fried fish, baked crabs and even sometimes, when available, roasted snipes!

The main course was served with a *"salaat"* or a suitable sauce and boiled vegetables on the side. Later, to add variety to our bland dinners, one of the Barooah cooks added shammi kebabs to the repertoire, serving it with chunky

finger chips and boiled vegetables to give it a Western touch! My sister learnt a new item in her school's cookery class – fish cakes. Not only was it a welcome change, it was delicious too.

The chop, cutlet, *dimmer* devil (scotch eggs), fish fry, *kabiraji* cutlet (derived from the word coverage, the fluffy batter encasing the cutlet) are considered colonial inventions. These items are very popular even today as snacks and may be found in small restaurants and hole-in-the-wall outlets strewn all over the city.

These ubiquitous food items may have had their origins in the Dalhousie area, the commercial hub. While the covenanted executives and brown sahibs sat down to Indo-British tiffins in comfortable lunch rooms, the clerks and the pen pushers had to scout for lunch on roadside cafes.

Dacres Lane is famous for its slew of mouth watering stews, chops and cutlets, cheap, delicious and filling. In fact, these items are  now part of the Bengali psyche and lifestyle. A chapter has been devoted to café food.

From the Rowland Road kitchen and my childhood memories, here then, are a few recipes.

─────── RECIPES ───────

Ma's Shammi Kababs

Serves four

Ingredients:

Meat (chicken or meat) – 500 gms (minced)
Chholar daal (chick pea) – 100gms
Onion – 1 medium (chopped)
Ginger – 1" (chopped)
Garlic – 2 cloves
Garam masala – 1 tsp
Cardamom – 1 big
Cinnamon – ½ inch (powdered)
Coriander and mint leaf – 1 bunch (chopped finely)
Lemon – 1
Green chilli – 2 (finely chopped)
White oil – 4 tbsp
Egg – 2
Salt – to taste

Method:

Boil mince meat, *daal and* garlic. Add salt, the mixture should be dry). Grind meat with *garam masala* to a fine paste. Add beaten egg gently and mix. Mixture should be dry enough to form balls. Mix, finely chopped onions, ginger, fresh coriander, mint and lemon juice, and set aside. Make patties out of the ground meat, fill with the salad mix in. Shape into round cakes, flatten and shallow fry. Serve with coriander leaves, onion rings and lemon slices.

Add gram flour to the meat paste if needed to thicken.

────────●────────

Didi's Fish Cakes

Serves four

Ingredients:

Bhetki fillet – 500 gms
Egg – 3, Potato – 4
Breadcrumb – 100 gms
Groundnut oil – 3 tbsp
Parsley/coriander or mint leaf – 2 tbsp (finely chopped)
Green chilli – 2 chopped (optional)
Lemon – 1 (sliced)
Milk – 2 tbsp, Butter – 1 tsp
Pepper – 1tsp, Salt – to taste

Method:

Boil fish with a pinch of salt. Boil, peel and mash potatoes with milk and butter. Mix potato, fish, beaten eggs, seasoning and herbs. Make flat round cakes, brush with ½ beaten egg coat cakes with breadcrumbs. Fry till golden.

Drain. Garnish with a sprigs of parsley or lemon slices.

Mesho's Lamb Chops

Serves four

Ingredients:

Meat rib chops – 8
Milk – 250 gms
Fennel/aniseed *(sauf/mouri)* – 2 tsp (paste), ½ tsp whole
Green chilli – 3 (chopped)
Ginger paste – 1 tsp
Chick pea flour *(besan)* – 2 tsp
White oil – 4 tbsp
Salt – to taste.

Method:

Boil or pressure cook chops in milk, ginger, aniseed paste and salt, till chops are done. Make a batter with chickpea flour add a few whole aniseeds and green chillies. Coat the chops with batter and fry chops till they are golden.

- Many years later, I realized the Kashmiri influence in this item.

Mamabarir Chingri Cutlet (prawn cutlet)

Serves four

Ingredients:

Prawn *(bagda)* – 12 (medium sized)
Ginger – ½ tbsp
Garlic paste – ½ tbsp
Lemon juice – 1 tsp
Turmeric powder/ paste – ½ tsp
Salt – to taste
Egg – 2 (beaten)
Breadcrumb – 2 tsp (heaped)
White oil – 3 tbsp
Flour – 1 tsp (if needed)

Method:

De-vein the prawns, remove heads and keep tails intact. Flatten prawns with a heavy spatula or a pestle, gently beating them till they are flat and round. Next marinate them in ginger and garlic paste and lemon juice. Add turmeric and salt. Keep for 1 hour. Gently dip one prawn at a time, in beaten egg, sprinkle with flour and coat with bread crumbs. Then fry prawns till crisp and golden.

Tips: To prepare chops and cutlets, use crumbled cornflakes or suji instead of breadcrumbs.

Rastar Nasta

— street treats

It was in the 1950's and 60's that Calcutta's street cafes began to acquire recognition and character. Bengali 'chop, cutlet, roast' at roadside cafes had began to surface in the early 20th century. Even after the British had departed the new avatars of colonial cuisine, appeared for the man on the street and were labeled 'Anglo-Indian' food. Long before that 'Moghlai' cuisine had been adapted by the Bengalis and served in local restaurants in the office areas.

Those who wished to sample more authentic continental food would do so in the elite clubs like the Calcutta Club, Bengal Club or the Saturday Club, or at the five star hotels such as The Grand, Spencer's, The Great Eastern Hotels or at select restaurants like Firpo's, Ferazzini's, Flury's, Mocambo and Skyroom. Only the well to do could indulge in this genre of western food, they were not pocket friendly to say the least. So what about the less affluent? Where would they sample food that was a bit exotic or foreign, but reasonably priced and also filling? Calcutta developed the art of 'snacks' or chop/ cutlets for the enjoyment of white collar workers, students and professionals at a price that suited their pockets.

The British memsahibs had taught the Indian cooks, to cook roasts and pies, chops and stews. Many versions of these items filtered down to ordinary citizens. Bengali cooks quickly adapted them to regional tastes. The humdrum Bengali kitchens did not have provisions for foreign food except the very rich zamindars, who had separate bawarchi khanas.

As Calcutta began to grow as a commercial hub, the city began to witness an inflow of a large migrant population. A multitude of daily commuters came to the city to work. Even to this day a vast majority of office workers arrives early in the morning to the metropolis by over-crowded

local trains. After office hours, they depart to their suburban homes. In between the floating tribe scouts for light refreshments to calm their rumbling stomachs. Lunch break is the time to stroll down to Esplanade or Dalhousie or Dacre's Lane (also now called Dekker's Lane) to savour a saucer of stew with a hunk of bread or bite into a spicy chop with a salad or a boiled egg sprinkled with salt and pepper on the side.

'Adda' (chinwag) time comes later, when friends meet, eat and chat. What goes better with a cup of steaming, sweet tea than chops or cutlets and hot gossip? Eating street food really meant slipping into a café by the wayside or what Bengalis call a 'cabin'. Simple wooden benches and marble or linoleum table tops, whirring fans, cigarette smoke and hum of voices are the signs of a typical café. Should couples seek privacy, curtained cabins are provided. The scene is typical. A cashier sits at the entrance shaking his legs. A simple black board provides a simple menu.

Café culture was as much for clerical workers as for intellectuals. Professors, scholars, artists and politicians frequented roadside, hole-in-the-wall eateries, where undisturbed over umpteen cups of

tea and snacks, ideas were exchanged with passion.

A well known writer, epicure, public relations persona and author of "Calcutta'a Street Cries" and "Fish and the Bengali", Late R P Gupta speaking to Harir Khobor of his memories of 50's street food, said "When we were young, food was the core of our *addas*. Coffee House 'adda*s' were an addiction, "cup after cup would be sipped, occasionally accompanied by toasts, sandwiches, omlettes etc. Discussions would be about cinemas, books, art and everything under the sun, even about the girl next door but the conversation invariably came back to food."

He said "Some evenings, we would head for Anadi Cabin near Esplanade for *Moghlais*, or to Chachar Cabin near Vivekananda's House for fowl and mutton cutlets, another day to Cafe de Monaco, famous for fish fries." His contemporaries longingly recall "*Gol Barir Kosha Mangsho*", Mitra Café's prawn cutlets, Niranjan's veg chops and liver fry. Mr Gupta shared his keenness for food with his friends Satyajit Ray, Kamal Majumdar, Kalishadhan Dasgupta, Kumar Mukherjee and Ranen Ray, intellectuals of the day.

He talked of mouth-watering whiffs from Gyan Babu's teashop of *Kobiraji* cutlets, mutton curry, the tempting aroma of Dilkhush Cabin's chops and even Hari Ghosh Street's 'banana

flower chops', that were sold on the pavement. It's interesting to note that the name *kabiraji*, comes from the word 'coverage', because the cutlets were covered in a frothy egg batter!

The chops, cutlets and even Moghlai parathas are even today served with a dollop of *kasundi* or mustard paste and shredded raw beet, carrot and onion salad.

Amongst Mr. Gupta's recollections of street food were, *ghoogni* flavoured with chopped mutton. Lip-smacking *alukabli* (spicy boiled lentils). "If one felt extravagant, one could indulge on *Chaamp* and *Roomali rooti* at

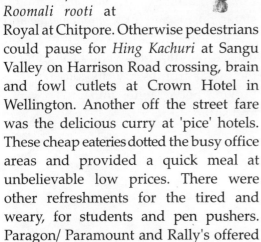

Royal at Chitpore. Otherwise pedestrians could pause for *Hing Kachuri* at Sangu Valley on Harrison Road crossing, brain and fowl cutlets at Crown Hotel in Wellington. Another off the street fare was the delicious curry at 'pice' hotels. These cheap eateries dotted the busy office areas and provided a quick meal at unbelievable low prices. There were other refreshments for the tired and weary, for students and pen pushers. Paragon/ Paramount and Rally's offered a formidable list of liquid refreshments. Chilled sherbets made with seasonal fruits, yoghurt and essences that soothed and satisfied parched throats.

"In the early 50's Nizam Hotel opened up a popular street delight. At first there were the kebabs later the famous *Calcutta kathi rolls* evolved." The rolls of thin, flat bread filled with spicy kebabs, garnished with lemon juice, onions and green chillies, are now ubiquitous. But in the 50's the Nizam's rolls were a novel treat. The 'rolls' were wolfed down after late night parties, cinema and drinking binges. It was fun to eat in cars parked on the street, with '*chhokra*' boys running to and fro and taking orders.

Walking down a street today, one may encounter cafés that offer 'roast chicken' and '*dimer devil*' (spice Scotch eggs) and meat filled 'patties'. Mr. Gupta ended his interview by saying that "Bengalis think and talk of food all the time. Even while walking they are tempted by wayside food, all the money goes on food!"

'*Chaats*' are a common wayside fast food. So are *phuchkas* and *chana garam*, not to mention the chowmein. Even seasonal cut fruit and roasted corn on the cob can be had on pavements. These cheap fillers are a boon. A variety of sweets are sold on Camac Street and Esplanade areas. From preserved fruit, '*beler morobbas, malpoa, sandesh, rosogollas* and *pithe*, give the passers by delicious respite from daily dru-dgery and hun-ger pangs.

———— RECIPES ————

Piaji (onion fritters)

Ingredients:

Onion – 200 gms (chopped)

Gram flour (besan) – 100 gms

Turmeric – a pinch

Green chilli – 2 (finely chopped)

Mustard oil – 100 gms

Salt to taste

Method:

Mix all ingredients together (except oil) and make a thick batter with water. Make cakes, deep fry in oil till golden brown. Serve with coriander or mint chutneys.

———— ◆◆ ————

Vegetable Chop

Ingredients:

Beetroot – 200 gms (boiled and mashed)

Carrots – 200 gms (boiled and mashed)

Potato – 200 gms (boiled and mashed)

Garam masala powder – a pinch

Raisin – 25 gms

Peanut – 25 gms

Flour – 2 tbsp (made into a batter)

Bread crumb – 150 gms

White oil – 200 gms

Salt and sugar – to taste

Method:

Mix all mashed vegetables, add salt and sugar, raisins and nuts, *garam masala* and fry. Cool the mixture. Form into round balls, dip in flour batter and roll them in the bread crumbs, fry till golden brown. Serve with mustard and salad.

Tips: Add few pieces old potatoes in the bread tin to keep bread fresh.

Alu Kabli (piquant potatoes)

Serves four

Ingredients:

Bengal gram – 200 gms (soaked and boiled)

Boiled potato – 2 large (peeled and diced)

Onion – 1 (finely chopped)

Tamarind pulp and jaggery – Mixed to make 2 tbsp of sauce

Cumin seed – ½ tsp (dry roasted and ground to a fine powder)

Salt – to taste

Method:

Toss all items together and serve.

Sprouted Chhola Chaat (a perennial roadside favourite)

Serves four

Ingredients:

Bengal gram – 200 gms (soaked overnight, then wrapped in a thin muslin cloth for a day to let shoots appear.)

Boiled potato – 200 gms (Pealed and diced)

Cucumber – ½ (diced)

Green chilli – ¾ (chopped)

Fresh ginger – ½" (diced fine)

Onion – 1 medium (chopped)

Lemon juice – 1 tsp

Coriander leaf – 2 tbsp

Balck salt – to taste

Method:

Mix all ingredients well and serve.

Baked Custard

Serves four

Ingredients:

Milk – ½ litre

Eggs – 3

Sugar – ¾ tbsp

Ground nutmeg/cinnamon

Method:

Warm the milk in a saucepan no need to boil. Whisk the eggs and sugar lightly in a basin, pour over the hot milk, stirring constantly to achieve a smooth texture.

Pour the mixture into a greased oven proof dish, sprinkle nutmeg or cinnamon powder on top and bake in the oven at 170C or microwave for about 35 to 45 minutes, till set and firm to the touch.

Note: The dish containing custard can be stood in a shallow tin containing water – this helps to ensure that the custard does not curdle.

OPTION: Make the custard and serve as a sauce with fresh or tinned fruit.

Roast Chicken a la roadside café

Serves four

Ingredients:

Chicken (cleaned) – 1 whole (1 kg)

Ghee or white oil – 1tbsp

Garam masala (whole) – 1 cinnamon (1"), 4 cardamoms, 4 cloves

Onion – 4 small (whole)

Ginger paste – 1 tbsp

Vinegar – 1 tbsp

Salt and black pepper – to taste

Method:

Tie the whole chicken tightly with string. Heat ghee or oil in a deep pan, add *garam masala* and onions, fry till brown. Add ginger paste, fry. Then add water, salt and pepper with chicken. Close lid. Let the chicken simmer in low fire. When chicken is tender, take out, slice and serve. The excess water in the pan can be stirred with a little flour and made into a gravy, pour this over chicken.

Spicy Meat Stew

Serves four

Ingredients:

Meat – 500 gms (cut into pieces)

Other ingredients as above

Carrot/ potatoes – 200 gms (optional)

Method:

same as above
Pressure cook. Serve with bread.

Moghlai Parota (moghlai parota)

Serves four

Ingredients:

Flour – 300 gms

Egg – 5

Onion – 150 gms (finely chopped)

Green chilli – 3 (finely chopped)

Black pepper – 1 tsp (powdered)

White oil – 200 gms

Ghee – 1 tbsp

Salt – to taste

Method:

Break eggs in a bowl, mix onion, green chillies, black pepper and salt beat well and keep aside. With flour, salt, ghee and water, make dough as for 'parota', cover with a wet cloth and set aside for ½ hour. Then roll out dough and make 10 squares. Lightly cook both sides in a frying pan or *tawa*, then pour 2 tbsp of the egg-mix in the middle of the *parota*, spread thinly. Next, fold the sides to form an envelope and seal. Gently add oil in the frying pan and fry both sides till golden brown.

Lal Jhaal Dim

— eggsactly red, hot!

It's a late night in October, and most everyone knows that it's not supposed to rain during the Pujas. But a burst of rain has temporarily pushed people under balconies, into the *pandals* and the less adventurous haven't left home at all. For a Bengali celebrating Durga Puja, this is a damp squib.

Maha Navami is the second last day of the Durga Puja festival, the night before *Bijoya* – the final and tenth day of the one celebration all Bengali Hindus live year round for.

Just past midnight, we amble into a side street next to the famous Jodhpur Park *puja*. We've convinced ourselves that the rain was a mere aberration, that all good Bengalis should venture out *pandal* crawling undaunted by the thundery skies. We are in a ritual search for the one thing tonight that would make the year memorable. No, it wasn't going to be one of the famous images of the Goddess Durga, or the decorations, or the faux architectural wonders of the *pandals*. We were in search of food. Post-drinks food.

Twenty five years on I still remember my good friend bending over a rather small *dekchi* (metal cooking pot) and exclaiming in delight. It was a small 'stall' we were at – not even a stall, just a charcoal oven (*unoon*) with a couple of *dekchis* of home made snacks. The vendor was selling *aalur dom* or dry potato curry, a few vegetables fries coated with chick pea flour (*piaji*), but wait…

Here we found Valhalla! Curried boiled eggs! Fried to a golden brown, the eggs were shining like amber from a bed of fiery red, gravy we call *jhol*. Bengalis cannot resist boiled eggs. *Sheddho dim* or boiled egg (specially when served with steaming hot ghee-drizzled rice) is a bit of an unwritten edict in Bengali culture.

Go to a cricket test match at the Eden Gardens in Calcutta, and about an hour or so into the wet but warming morning, you'll see across the aisle the inevitable appearance of the Bengali custom of snacking on boiled eggs. Garnished

with a sprinkling of salt and ground black pepper wrapped in an ear panel of the *Ananda Bazar Patrika*. That's about when the second England wicket falls. Thirteen overs have been bowled. And the mildly whiffy, oh-so-tempting, somewhat pungent aroma of the hard boiled egg, split in half and tempered with ground black pepper, is in the air, being contentedly munched on as the balls whizz about.

Those eggs at the *puja pandal* stall – and we counted them thrice – there were fourteen, sometimes thirteen, and on one count just eleven (our friend Babun had had a wee dram too many of the other Bengali favourite, the tipple necessary to wash down the *puja* celebrations back then in the 1990s – Old Monk rum) – those eggs looked hot. And hot, not just in a spicy way, but in a mouth watering, greed-inducing way that wasn't just about taste. Every sense was involved in the desperate hunger-induced frenzy that followed soon.

The four of us demolished those *dims* (eggs) in the next few minutes. Hungry at first, the early ones just went down in a rapid fire burst of gluttony. Then we licked the red paste that was nowhere near a *jhol* but more a murderous slang of spices simmered into a perfect texture of crimson gold evil. This was an experience. These were gems we savoured and shared then wiped our fingers across the *dekchi* and cleaned up. Twenty five years on, whenever we meet and talk about good times, there's one thing that always comes up. *The Lal Jhaal Dim.*

There's a perfect way to boil the egg that Shadhon the vendor knew of (we quickly made friends with him, his wife Ratna and his nephew Terra or the squint-eyed one). So here it is: three or four minutes after the water (with the eggs) is bubbling large and proud, simmer it down for another two minutes. Then drain the water and wash the eggs in cold water. The egg for the perfect *sheddho dim* should almost be over boiled. You can't essentially go wrong on a classic Bengali hard boiled egg. Peel. And then go about transforming the humble boiled egg into Lal Jhaal Dim.

---------- RECIPES ----------

Lal Jhal Dim

Serves four

Ingredients:

Egg – 8	
Red chilli powder/ paste – 1 ½ tsp	
Garlic – 2 tsp	
Onion – 4 tbsp (finely chopped)	
Lemon – 1	
Salt – to taste	

Method:

Boil and peel the eggs as above. Make cuts on the whites with a sharp knife. Make a paste of salt, red chilli paste, garlic. Fill in the cuts with this paste, fry lightly in mustard oil. Cut the egg length wise, sprinkle with raw onions and a squeeze of lemon. Serve.

Bangladesher Khawa
– a culinary expedition

> "*I should like to rise and go...*
> *where in sunshine reaching out*
> *Eastern cities, miles about*
> *Are with mosque and minarets*
> *Away sandy gardens set*
> *And rich goods from near and far*
> *Many for sale in the bazaar*"
>
> — Robert Louis Stevenson

From Sealdah Station we took a train to Bongaon, and headed for Petrapole. Then we walked across to Benapole, the check post of Bangladesh. On the way to Dhaka our destination, we passed through Satkheera, Jessore and Faridpur, the original birthplaces and hometowns of many displaced Bengali families.

On the way to Dhaka, we passed vast stretches of paddy fields, numerous canals, rivers, ponds and marshes. The thatched huts, the cotton and *palash* trees laden with crimson flowers, the calls of the cuckoo and the bulbul were reminiscent of our countryside in West Bengal. Once, we were an undivided nation. How could the scenery be different? The difference was in the clothes, habits and customs. The village folk, no longer wear traditional *lungis* (wrap around sarongs) and dhotis. The men folk have adopted the Arabic jelebias! We noticed Bengali villagers lounging around thatched cottages, in middle eastern robes, heads covered in turbans. Is the influence of religion so strong that in the heat of a mid-summer afternoon the native of Bengal, fed on flattened and popped rice, keeps himself cool by donning Arabic robes instead of a lungi or dhoti? In Dhaka I realize that the Bengali of Bangladesh has forsaken the plain or puffed rice and even fish. Rich and heavily spiced kebabs, biryanis, pulaos and firnis have replaced plain dal, jhol and simple mix of vegetables.

Soon, the bus stopped at the Aricha pier near Goalando. The magnificent Padma River gleamed before us. The ferry waited on the wharf to take us to Dhaka. We watched the sun set and the full moon rise over the waters of the Padma. Tiny lamps, from dargahs danced on the waves alongside our ferry. An unforgettable sight.

We arrived in Dhaka hungry and tired. The hotel's Chinese restaurant produced a reasonably cooked Red Snapper, served with steamed vegetables, which we hungrily devoured. We discovered that Dhaka had numerous Thai and Chinese restaurants, scattered around the posh areas.

The next day we set off, eager to taste the bespoke *Dhakai parathas* and freshly fried fish by the ferry wharf.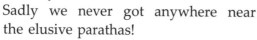
Sadly we never got anywhere near the elusive parathas!

East Bengal was a gourmet's paradise, so we were told, we were looking forward eagerly to a meal of fresh fish in this land of fish. We planned to taste the local food everywhere, be it in the hill tracts of Chittagong, the Chakma homeland or even St. Martin's, the tiny coral island in the Bay of Bengal.

Alas, all we could see were signs for chicken *pulao*, chicken *jhalfry* and kebabs.

Finally we settled for *birani* out of sheer hunger and desperation, when we chanced upon a famous *birani* (Bangladeshi name for Biryani) shop.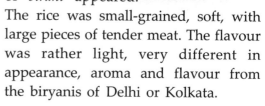

Steaming plates of *birani* appeared. The rice was small-grained, soft, with large pieces of tender meat. The flavour was rather light, very different in appearance, aroma and flavour from the biryanis of Delhi or Kolkata.

Biryanis are of two kinds, *kachchi* and *pakki*. In the latter the meat is cooked separately till it is half done then the rice is added. In *kachchi* biryani, the meat and rice are cooked together. This is a more difficult process and, according to Bangaladeshi chefs, only experienced hands can perfect it. Undaunted we pleaded for recipes, which I quickly jotted down.

Next day we moved on to Chittagong. The hilly tracts in the foothills of tea growing slopes. The Rangamati river flows through the city and meets the sea. Along the coast is the longest beach in the world, and is famous for its landmark Cox's Bazaar. Incidentally the cooks of Chittagong are famous for their culinary crafts, originally known as 'Mugs', they arrived in the bustling city of old Calcutta to be trained by British memsahibs to produce stews, pies, roasts, puddings and cakes! These were the cooks who mastered the art of de-boning the Hilsa and smoking the fillets over wood fire. Thus, we were looking forward to sampling various epicurean delights in this city. We were lucky, Jehangir Jabbar, a friend, invited us home for dinner.

At last we would sample authentic Bangladesh food. We were not disappointed, dish after dish arrived at the table we tasted chunky pieces of hilsa, carp, climbing perch, chital, prawns in coconut gravy and goat meat curry! The repast was lavish beyond words. Bangladeshis are generous hosts and nothing is spared. There were six or seven items of assorted dishes of meat, fish and poultry. All cooked with care – a veritable feast. However, the dishes had a Moghlai touch. Except for one or two fish items, the style of cooking was not typical Bengali. Where did the vegetables disappear? The only two vegetarian items were, Pulao made with small grained rice and fried brinjal. The dinner was rounded off with home made sweet curds and sweetmeats All in all it was a novel experience. Something to write home about. I jotted down a few recipes gleaned from the cook for *Harir Khobor*.

We returned to Dhaka, and the next day we drove to Narayangunj, one of the main centres of the textile industry in Bangladesh. Bikrampur and Narayangunj have always been prosperous cities. Many ancient Hindu zamindar families lived here.

In Narayangunj we spend part of a day as guests of a wealthy business family and noted with interest their manners and customs. The lady of the house wore a burkha and spoke gently from behind the veil. Traditional women do not appear without the veil in front of strangers, specially men. The lady of the house, was a wonderful hostess. She had cooked and supervised the entire meal. Each and every item was superb.

After lunch, when the men folk were taking a stroll. I was allowed to chat with our hostess in her bedroom. I persuaded the petite and cheerful lady to take off her severe veil, over gossip and tea, I coaxed her to share her recipe book with me. From her book I selected two recipes – *Morag Polao* and *Dariai Kabab*, – which we had just relished at lunch, and two others, *Ilish Machher Tauk Salan* and *Semai Jarda*.

——— RECIPES ———

Koi Machher Do Piaza (climbing perch in onion gravy)

Serves four

Ingredients:

Climbing Perch – 8 (medium sized)

Turmeric paste – 1 tsp

Onion – ½ cup (chopped), 2tbsp (paste)

Garlic paste – 2 ½ tsp

Coriander powder/ paste – 2 tsp

Cumin powder/ paste – 2 tsp

Red chilli powder/ paste – 1 tsp

Mustard oil – 100 gms

Salt – to taste

Method:

Smear the fish with salt and turmeric, fry lightly and keep aside.

Fry chopped onions till brown and crisp, keep aside.

Now fry onion and garlic pastes. Add rest of the spices and fry. Add fried fish and salt. Pour half a cup of water, cover and cook till fish is done and the gravy is thick. Garnish with fried onions.

Kachchi Biryani

Serves four

Ingredients:

Basmati rice – 500 gms

Meat – 1 kg (large pieces)

Yoghurt – 500 gms (beaten)

Onion paste – 4 tbsp

Ginger paste – 2 tbsp

Saffron – 1 tsp

Cardamom – 6 (whole)

Clove – 8 (whole)

Cinnamon – 5 (1"each)

Coriander powder/ paste – 2 tbsp

Oil or ghee – 250 gms

Salt – to taste

Method:

Extract juice from the ginger. Soak saffron in water. Make a paste of the saffron and cardamom. Marinate the pieces of meat in the onion and coriander pastes, ginger juice and salt for 1½ hours. Combine yoghurt and saffron-cardamom paste and add to the marinated mutton. Set aside for 30 minutes.

Take a large, heavy-gauge vessel and arrange the rice and meat in layers.

Top with cloves, cinnamon, oil, ghee and required amount of water. Cover the vessel and seal the edges with a thick paste made of flour. Cook on low heat till done.

Begum Husne Ara's Dariai Kabab (meat kebabs) | Serves four

Ingredients:

Meat (boneless) – 1 kg (cubed)

Onion – 500 gms

Yoghurt – 250 gms

Saffron – a little

Ginger paste – 2 tbsp

Egg – 7

Coriander seed – 100 gms

Peppercorn – 8 (whole)

Cinnamon stick – 4 (whole)

Cardamom – 4 (whole)

Clove – 4 (whole)

Groundnut oil – 250 gms

Salt – to taste

Method:

Mix saffron with water, half of the yoghurt and 100 gms oil and keep aside. Marinate the meat in ginger paste, salt and the remaining yoghurt for 2 hours.

Grind the coriander, peppercorns, cinnamon, cardamoms and cloves to a paste. Boil the eggs and slice them into thick rounds. Chop half of the onions finely; cut the rest into cubes. Heat oil, fry chopped onions, add half the spice paste and fry. Add marinated meat and fry till done. Remove from fire and mix with rest of the spice pastes.

Pierce egg pieces, onion cubes and meat alternately on skewers. Grill over a low flame, basting with saffron-curd-oil mixture. Serve with coriander chutney.

Begum's Ilish Machher Tauk Salan (hilsa with lemon) | Serves four

Ingredients:

Hilsa fish – 1 kg (without head or tail)

Green chilli – 6 (seeded & chopped)

Lemon juice – 1 tbsp

Mustard oil – 150 gms

Salt – to taste

Method:

Arrange hilsa pieces in a pan. Smear the fish with salt, lemon juice, green chillies and oil. Marinate for 20 minutes.

Add water and put the pan on heat. Bring to boil, cover and simmer till the fish is done.

Begum Husne Ara's Morag Pulao (chicken in rice)

| Serves four

Ingredients:

Fine rice – 500 gms

Chicken – 1 kg (cut in large pieces)

Pistachio – 4 (soaked & chopped)

Almond – 4 (soaked & chopped)

Saffron – ¼ tsp

Keora (screwpine flower) water – ¼ tsp

Yoghurt – 4 tbsp

Nutmeg – ½ tsp (grated)

Cardamom – 2 (whole), 1 tsp (paste)

Onion paste – 4 tbsp, 4 tbsp (chopped)

Garlic paste – 1 tbsp

Coriander paste – 2 tbsp

Ginger paste – 2 tbsp

Cinnamon stick – 2 (1"each)

Milk – 1 cup

Thickened milk *(khoya)* – 100 gms

Groundnut oil – 200 gms

Ghee – 2 tbsp

Raisin – 25 gms (soaked in water)

Lemon wedges – for garnish

Salt & sugar – to taste

Method:

Make a paste of saffron with *keora* water. Dissolve *khoya* in a cup of milk and keep aside. Fry chopped onions and keep aside. Wash rice and drain well.

Marinate chicken with yoghurt, salt, sugar, nutmeg, cardamom powder, onion, garlic, coriander, saffron and ginger, with a tsp of oil, for two hours. Cover the vessel and cook over low heat till the chicken is half-done and dry.

Heat oil in a large pan and fry whole cinnamon and cardamoms for a minute and then add rice, fry a little, add salt and sugar, pour water, cook till half done and dry.

Now in another pan arrange half done rice and chicken pieces in layers. Sprinkle water and *khoya* mix, *keora* water, raisins, almonds, pistachios and ghee. Cover with a tight lid and simmer till done. Garnish with fried onions and serve with lemon wedges.

Tips:

- Place pieces of charcoal in the refrigerator, to keep away stale odour and prevent fungus.
- Wash the ice tray with hot water to ease out ice cubes.

Begum Husne Ara's Semai (spiced vermicelli dessert)
Serves four

Ingredients:

Vermicelli – 500 gms

Water – 6/7 cups

Sugar – 2 cups

Bay leaf – 5

Peppercorn – a few

Cardamom – 10

Cinnamon stick – 6 (1" sticks)

Ginger paste – 2 tsp

Cottage cheese – 200 gms (paste)

Raisins – 25 gms (soaked)

Cashew nut – 12

Almond – 1 tsp (powdered)

Pistachio – 1 tsp (powdered)

Groundnut oil – ½ cup

Salt – a pinch

Method:

Fry vermicelli in oil till it golden, drain and keep aside. Now boil water, sugar, bay leaves, peppercorns, cardamoms, ginger, cinnamon sticks and salt in a pan till a syrupy consistency, blend in the vermicelli and cottage cheese.

After liquid has evaporated, add the raisins and the whole and powdered nuts. Mix well and remove from fire.

Glossary

Cereals

English	Bengali	Hindi
Basmati rice	Basmati chaal	Basmati chawal
Flattened or beaten rice	Chirey	Chura/ poha
Flour	Moida	Maida
Popped rice	Khoi	Khoi
Popped rice with jaggery	Murki	Murki
Puffed rice	Moori	Moori
Rice	Chaal	Chawal
Rice (boiled)	Bhaat	Bhaat
Rice flour	Chaaler guro	Chawal atta
Semolina	Sooji	Sooji
Wheat flour	Aatta	Aatta

Edible Flowers

English	Bengali	Hindi
Banana flower	Mocha	Kele ka phul
Drumstick flower	Sajney phul	Sajina phul
Flower	Phul	Phul
Pumpkin flowers	Kumror phul	Kaddu ka phul
Sesbania flower	Bok phul	—

Edible oils

English	Bengali	Hindi
Groundnut oil	Badam tel	Badam tel
Mustard oil	Shorshey tel	Sarson ki tel
Oil	Tel	Tel
Soyabean oil	Soyabean tel	Soyabean tel
Sunflower oil	Surjamukhi tel	—
White oil (groundnut/ sunflower)	Sada tel	Sada tel

Fish and Crustaceans

English	Bengali	Hindi
Beckti / Asian Seabass	Bhetki	Bhetki machchi
Bombay duck	Loita mach	—
Carp	Rui/ Mrigel/ Katla	Rohu/ Mirgel/ Katla
Cat fish	Magur/ Shinghi/ Tangra/ Aar	Magur/ Shinghi/ Tangra/ Aar
Climbing perch	Koi	—
Clown Knifefish	Chital	Chital
Crab	Kankra	Kankra
Crayfish	Golda chingri	Jhinga
Fish	Machh	Machchi
Gangetic Ailia	Kajli mach	—
Hilsa	Illish	Hilsha machchi
Indian butter fish	Pabda	Pupta
Indian salmon	Gurjali mach	Ravas
Mango fish	Topse mach	Topsi
Mola carplet/ white bait	Mourala	Morolla
Mullet	Parshey	Boi
Murrel	Shole	Shole
Prawn	Bagda chingri	Jhinga
Roe	Machher dim	Machchi ka anda
Shrimp	Kucho chingri	Jhinga
Sprat	Kachki	—
Tank Goby	Bele	—

◆◆

Fried breads

English	Bengali	Hindi
Bread	Pau rooti	Pau rooti
Fried flatbread	Parota	Paratha
Fried flatbread patty	Moglai parota	Moglaip paratha
Fried flour bread	Luchi	Luchi
Patty with fillings	Kochuri	Kochuri
Savoury bits	Nimki	Namkin

Fruits & nuts

English	Bengali	Hindi
Bcashew	Kaju badam	Kaju
Coconut	Narkel	Nariyal
Fruit	Phal	Phal
Green mango	Kancha aam	Aam
Indian plum	kool	Ber
Lemon	Lebu	Nimbu
Mango	Aam	Aam
Nut	Badam	Badam
Orange	Kamala lebu	Santra
Peanut	Chine badam	Mung phalli
Pineapple	Anaras	Anaras
Pistachio	Pesta	Pista
Raisin	Kismis	Kismis
Tamarind	Tentul	Imli
Watermelon	Tormuj	Tarbuj
Wood apple	Bael	Shree phal

◆◆

Greens

English	Bengali	Hindi
Aquatic Greens/ water spinach	Kalmi shaak	Katha saag
Climbing spinach	Pui shaak	—
Coriander leaf	Dhoney pata	Dhaniya patta
Fenugreek green	Methi shaak	Methi saag
Fiddlehead	Dhaki shaak	—
Greens	Shaak	Saag
Leafy stems of gourd/ pumpkin	Lau/ kumro shaak	—
Margosa leaf	Neem pata	Neem patti
Mint leaf	Pudina pata	Pudina
Mustard greens	Shorshey shaak	Sarson ki saag
Parval leaf	Palta pata	—
Pea greens	Matar shaak	Matar saag
Red spinach	Lal shaak	Lal saag
Spinach	Paalang shaak	Palak
Taro Runners	Kochur loti	—
Taro stalks	Kochu shaak	Ghuiyan saag

Lentils

English	Bengali	Hindi
Bengal gram	Chhola	Chhana
Chick pea/ gram flour	Besan	Besan
Chick peas	Kabuli chhola	Kabuli chhana
Dried lentil balls	Bori	Bori
Lentil	Daal	Daal
Red lentils	Mushur daal	Masoor
Split Bengal gram	Chholar daal	Chhana daal
Split black lentils	Kalai daal	Urad dal
Split green gram	Moog/ sona moog daal	Moong daal
Split pea lentils	Matar daal	Matar daal
Split pigeon pea flour	Chatu	Chattu
Split pigeon pea lentils	Arhar daal	Toor/ toovar dal
Yellow pea	Matar	Matar

◆◆

Meat and Poultry

English	Bengali	Hindi
Chicken/ fowl	Murgi	Murgh
Egg	Dim	Aanda
Meat	Mangsho	Gosht/ bakri
Mince/ ground meat	Keema	Keema
Mutton/ lamb	Bherar mangsho	Bheri

◆◆

Milk product

English	Bengali	Hindi
Clarified butter	Ghee	Ghee
Cottage cheese	Chhana	Chhenna
Rice pudding	Payesh	Kheer
Thickened milk	Khoya kheer	Khoya
Yoghurt	Doi	Dahi
Yogurt drink/ shake	Ghole	Lassi

Spices

English	Bengali	Hindi
Aniseed/ fennel	Mouri	Saunf
Asafoetida	Hing	Hing
Bay leaf	Tej pata	Tej patta
Black cardamom	Boro elach	Bara elaichi
Black cumin seed	Shah jeera	Shah jeera
Black pepper	Gol morich	Kala mirch
Black salt	Beet noon	Kala namak
Carom seeds	Jowan	Ajwain
Cinamon	Daruchini	Dalchini
Cloves	Labongo	lavang
Coriander seed	Dhoney	Dhania
Cumin seed	Sada jeera	Jeera
Dried mango powder	Aamchur	Aamchur
Dried red chilli	Shukno lanka	Sukha lal mirich
Fenugreek seeds	Methi	Methi dana
Five spice (aniseed, cumin, fenugreek, mustard and onion seed)	Panch phoron	Panch phoron
Cloves, cinnamon & green cardamoms (whole)	Garam masala	Garam masala
Garlic	Rasoon	Lasoon
Ginger	Aada	Adrak
Green cardamom	Choto elach	Elaichi
Green chilli	Kancha lanka	Hara mirch
Mace	Jaitri	Javitri
Mustard seeds	Shorshey	Sarson
Nutmeg	Jaiphal	Jaiphal
Onion seed	Kalo jeera	Kala jeera
Poppy seeds	Posto	Khus khus
Saffron	Jafran	Jafran/ keshar
Salt	Noon/ laban	Namak
Seeds of Indian parley	Radhuni	—
Sesame seed	Til	Til
Spice	Masla	Masale
Turmeric	Halud	Haldi

Vegetables

English	Bengali	Hindi
Arum	Ole	Kaddu
Beetroot	Beet	Beet
Bitter gourd	Korela/ uchchhe	Karela
Brinjal	Begun	Baigan
Broad bean	Seem	Sheem
Cabbage	Bandha kopi	Bandgobi
Carrot	Gajor	Gajar
Cauliflower	Phulkopi	Gobi
Cucumber	Sasha	Kheera
Drumstick	Sajne danta	Sajina danta
Gourd	Lau	Lauki
Green jackfruit	Enchor	Kancha kanthal
Green papaya	Pepey	Papita
Green peas	Matarshuti	Hara matar
Horse radish	Mulo	Muli
Jackfruit seed	Kanthal bichi	Kanthal ka beej
Okra	Dhanros	Bhindi
Onion	Piaj	Piaj
Parwal	Potol	Parwal
Peels	Khosha	Chhilke
Pith of plantain stems	Thor	Kele-ki-tana
Potato	Aalu	Aalu
Raw banana	Kanch Kala	Kacha kela
Red pumpkin	Kumro	Kaddu
Ridge gourd	Jhingey	Torai
Sweet potato	Ranga aalu	Shakarkhand
Taro	Kochu	Ghuiyan
Tomato	Tometo	Tamatar
Vegetables	Kancha torkari	Sabji